CAMBRIDGE TEXTS IN THE
HISTORY OF POLITICAL THOUGHT

=

JEREMY BENTHAM
A Fragment on Government

CAMBRIDGE TEXTS IN THE
HISTORY OF POLITICAL THOUGHT

Series Editors:

RAYMOND GEUSS *Columbia University*
QUENTIN SKINNER *Christ's College, Cambridge*
RICHARD TUCK *Jesus College, Cambridge*

The series is intended to make available to students the most important texts required for an understanding of the history of political thought. The scholarship of the present generation has greatly expanded our sense of the range of authors indispensable for such an understanding, and the series will reflect those developments. It will also include a number of less well-known works, in particular those needed to establish the intellectual contexts that in turn help to make sense of the major texts. The principal aim, however, will be to produce new versions of the major texts themselves, based on the most up-to-date scholarship. The preference will always be for complete texts, and a special feature of the series will be to complement individual texts, within the compass of a single volume, with subsidiary contextual material. Each volume will contain an introduction on the historical identity and contemporary significance of the text concerned.

Among the first titles in the series will be:

Aristotle, *edited by Stephen Everson*
Cicero, *edited by Miriam Griffin*
Seneca, *edited by John Cooper*
Ockham, *edited by A. S. McGrade*
Machiavelli, *edited by Quentin Skinner and Russell Price*
More, *edited by George Logan*
Luther and Calvin, *edited by Harro Höpfl*
Bodin, *edited by Julian H. Franklin*
Hooker, *edited by A. S. McGrade*
Vindiciae contra tyrannos, *edited by George Garnett*
Grotius, *edited by Richard Tuck*
Milton, *edited by Martin Dzelzainis*
Pufendorf, *edited by James Tully*
Leibniz, *edited by Patrick Riley*
Locke, *edited by Peter Laslett*
Kant, *edited by Hans Reiss*
Diderot, *edited by John Hope Mason and Robert Wokler*
Constant, *edited by Biancamaria Fontana*
Fourier and Saint-Simon, *edited by Gareth Stedman Jones*
Hegel, *edited by Allen Wood*
Marx, *edited by Terrell Carver and Joseph O'Malley*
Critical Theory, *edited by Raymond Geuss*
Montesquieu, *edited by Anne Cohler et al.*

JEREMY BENTHAM

A Fragment on Government

THE NEW
AUTHORITATIVE EDITION BY
J. H. BURNS
AND
H. L. A. HART

WITH AN INTRODUCTION BY
ROSS HARRISON
*University Lecturer in Philosophy
and Fellow of King's College, Cambridge*

The right of the
University of Cambridge
to print and sell
all manner of books
was granted by
Henry VIII in 1534.
The University has printed
and published continuously
since 1584.

CAMBRIDGE UNIVERSITY PRESS
CAMBRIDGE
NEW YORK   NEW ROCHELLE
MELBOURNE   SYDNEY

Published by the Press Syndicate of the University of Cambridge
The Pitt Building, Trumpington Street, Cambridge CB2 1RP
32 East 57th Street, New York, NY 10022, USA
10 Stamford Road, Oakleigh, Melbourne 3166, Australia

This edition of *A Fragment on Government* was first published as
part of *The Collected Works of Jeremy Bentham* in 1977,
in the volume (edited by J.H. Burns and H.L.A. Hart) containing
A Comment on the Commentaries and *A Fragment on Government*
© University of London 1977.

© in the introduction and new editorial matter
Cambridge University Press

First published 1988

Printed in Great Britain by
Redwood Burn Ltd, Trowbridge, Wiltshire

British Library cataloguing in publication data
Bentham, Jeremy, 1748–1832
Jeremy Bentham: *A Fragment on Government.–*
(Cambridge texts in the history of political thought).
1. Government
I. Title   II. Burns, J.H. (James Henderson), 1921–
III. Hart, H.L.A. (Herbert Lionel Adolphus), 1907–
350

Library of Congress cataloguing in publication data
Bentham, Jeremy, 1748–1832
Jeremy Bentham: *A Fragment on Government.* Jeremy Bentham.–
New authoritative ed. by J.H. Burns and H.L.A. Hart;
with an introduction by Ross Harrison.   p.   cm.–
(Cambridge texts in the history of political thought)
Bibliography.
Includes index.
ISBN 0 521 35054 9   ISBN 0 521 35929 5 (pbk)
1. Utilitarianism.   2. Blackstone, William, Sir, 1723–1780.
Commentaries on the laws of England.
3. Law–Philosophy. 1921–   4. Political science
I. Burns, J.H. (James Henderson), 1921–
II. Hart, H.L.A. (Herbert Lionel Adolphus), 1907– .
III. Title. IV. Series.
K334.B444 1988
340′.1–dc19   88–1729 CIP

ISBN 0 521 35054 9 hard covers
ISBN 0 521 35929 5 paperback

Contents

Introduction

In his own copy of the *Fragment on Government*, Jeremy Bentham made the handwritten note that 'this was the very first publication by which men at large were invited to break loose from the trammels of authority and ancestor-wisdom on the field of law'. It is a young man's book. It is a fresh book, fresh with energy, ideas, and hope. It is a critical book, surveying the established and uncongenial world and determined to show how it might do better. The legal and political world is to be constructed anew from first principles. As Bentham noted in a manuscript written shortly after the *Fragment*, he had found, on commencing study of the law, 'the various rights and duties of the various classes of mankind jumbled together in one immense and unsorted heap: men ruined for not knowing what they are neither enabled nor permitted to learn: and the whole fabric of jurisprudence a labyrinth without a clew'. The only way he saw to 'cleanse the Augean stable' was 'to pour in a body of severe and steady criticism and to spread it over the whole extent of the subject in one comprehensive unbroken tide'. So the current state of the law he took to be a mass of filth – in another place he commented that training in the law was like being asked to roll in the contents of a night cart – and this all had to be flushed away by new thought and new criticism. Bentham thought that he had found the clew to the labyrinth – the thread which would guide him into understanding of the law – and could recreate law and political theory from shiny, rational, first principles.

The *Fragment* is a confident work. It is more concerned with criticism than construction, with flushing out the stables than building the new palace; yet the foundations for the constructive thought are laid here. In both criticism and creation, the confidence stems from Bentham's feeling that history is on his side. As he puts it at the start of the work, 'The age we live in is a busy age; in which knowledge is rapidly advancing towards perfection.' The secrets have been found, the methods and fundamental truths have been discovered. They only need now to be applied in an age impatient for improvement and reform. Central among these foundational truths is the 'fundamental axiom', also declared on the first page of the work, that '*it is the greatest happiness of the greatest number that is the measure of right and wrong*'. With this basis, the theory and practice of both politics and law can be reconstructed from first principles. The aim, as he puts it at the start of his next book, the *Introduction to the Principles of Morals and Legislation*, is 'to rear the fabric of felicity by the hands of reason and of law'. Felicity, happiness, is the end. Reason and law are the means. Creating correct law will lead to happiness; and the creation of correct law means reasoning from first principles rather than adopting the piled up rubbish of ancient authority.

Criticism needs a target and the *Fragment* has a highly specific one. As the subtitle says, it is the examination of what is 'delivered, on the subject of government in general in the Introduction to Sir William Blackstone's Commentaries'. Sir William Blackstone was a lawyer and his *Commentaries* were legal commentaries. In choosing Blackstone as his target Bentham was intentionally choosing the foremost legal writer of his day. If the current rubbish was to be removed then Blackstone, its foremost expositor and defender in the public eye, had to go. Yet Bentham here directs his criticism not to the main work of legal exposition, nor even to his introductory account of the general nature of law, but to a largely irrelevant small portion of this introduction, the portion on government in general. Since Bentham, particularly at this time, was more interested in law than politics, the *Fragment* would seem to be peripheral to Bentham's central concerns. It also seems to be of disproportionate length. The whole of the *Fragment* is an examination of a mere seven pages of Blackstone's original thousand-page work. If the Augean stables are to be cleared at this rate, even Hercules might have found it beyond him, and it hardly leaves time for subsequent reconstruction. It is not the tempo suggested by the claim that knowledge is rapidly advancing towards perfection.

Appearances, however, are deceptive. The *Fragment* should not be thought of as merely a small part of a commentary on Blackstone, let alone as a single barrowload of filth removed from the mountains in the stables. Blackstone's esteem made him a useful target and this portion of his *Commentaries*, central or otherwise, gave Bentham the chance to show how everything could be done better when reworked from first principles. So the *Fragment* should be looked at as an illustrative sample, a sample both of the way in which things should not be done and also of the way in which they should be done. It might have been about this part of Blackstone, it might have been about another; and it is also the case that Bentham works in some of his objections to other parts of Blackstone's text in passing.

The *Fragment* is self-declared in its title to be only a fragment, a portion wrenched from a larger work; and Bentham explains in the Preface why this is so. Engaged in writing a commentary on the introductory sections of Blackstone, he came upon a digression and so decided to separate his commentary on it from his commentary on the rest. Yet what Bentham does not explain is that writing on Blackstone was itself a digression from his main project, largely caused by accidental circumstances. So the *Fragment* is not just a fragment, but the fragment of a fragment; not just a digression, but a digression from a digression. There is an onion of indirection here which must now be peeled by saying more about the two parties to the conflict, Blackstone and Bentham.

The target of the *Fragment*, Sir William Blackstone, was not only well known in his day but still has a reputation as a legal commentator. He had had a fairly standard, but largely unsuccessful, legal career before he took the advice of the great judge, Lord Mansfield, and decided to give private lectures at Oxford. These lectures, which started in 1753, were a great success and Blackstone was subsequently made the first Vinerian Professor of Law at Oxford, continuing to give the same course of lectures. Giving lectures on law, particularly by a professor of the subject, might seem to be an unremarkable activity. However, when Blackstone did it, it was quite exceptional. Both at the ancient universities and at the Inns of Court in London, the practice of giving any formal instruction in the law had quite died out. Indeed, even when there had been formal instruction at the ancient universities it had been in roman and canon law, and Blackstone's lectures were the first on the laws of England ever given in an English university. So, lacking formal instruction, aspiring lawyers learned their trade by observing the law in practice, either by watching it being made and applied by the judges sitting in Westminster Hall or by working for a practising attorney.

Blackstone believed that these haphazard methods should be supplemented by a much more formal legal education, and the value of such an education is a theme of his inaugural lecture, reprinted as section one of the Introduction to his *Commentaries*. However, talking to the young gentlemen of Oxford, he was not really in a position to do much about this, and education in the law, such as it was not, continued much the same as before. It is true that some of his audience, such as the young Bentham who attended the course in 1763, did intend to become practising lawyers. Yet the future contact with the law of most of the young gentlemen of Oxford was to be in a purely amateur capacity, either as local magistrates or else as members of parliament enacting statutes. It was particularly this latter group which Blackstone had as his target in his inaugural lecture, attacking the confusions produced in the largely judge-made common law by parliamentary legislation. What Blackstone wanted to do, therefore, was to produce a clear and organised account of the law which gave an understanding of its content for outsiders and amateurs. In Bentham's words, as printed here, he taught law to speak 'the language of the Scholar and the Gentleman' (23). Bentham is himself echoing Blackstone who says in the inaugural lecture that 'a competent knowledge of the laws of that society in which we live is the proper accomplishment of every gentleman and scholar'.

Although unprecedented, the lectures were very successful and copies made by the students began to circulate. Blackstone therefore determined to put them into print himself and so arose the famous *Commentaries*, which appeared in four volumes starting in 1765. Beautifully written, the *Commentaries* gave Blackstone the reputation which he had formerly sought in vain while practising the law, and he returned to high legal office in London. They were also, in fact, extensively used by aspiring lawyers and so, rather than being merely an ornament for gentlemen, proved to have enduring significance in general legal education, particularly in America. Over twenty editions had appeared by the middle of the nineteenth century.

Blackstone's aim in the *Commentaries* was to outline the current law of England. He was not, therefore, particularly interested in government, that is in such questions as whether or not there should be government, what form it should take, or what, if any, was the legitimate foundation of obedience. Government in general, and the government of England in particular, was something which for his purposes he could easily have taken for granted. However, law does presuppose government and so, perhaps because Blackstone felt that he had an obligation as a scholar to say something about it, before he starts the main work he deals with the question of the general nature of law and government in introductory sections. In any case, he thought that this presented him with no particular problems as the answers to such questions as the origin and validity of government or of the excellence of the British constitution lay ready to hand. So, after reprinting the inaugural lecture, he devoted the second section of the introduction to 'the nature of laws in general' and, in the course of it, lifted a rather muddled version of why government was a good thing from contemporary apologetics. It is this small secondary part of the work that was seized on by Bentham and worried remorselessly in the text printed here.

It can be seen from this that Blackstone was not in fact an arch conservative, trying to defend every aspect of current legal thought or practice, and that Bentham was in any case attacking him on a sector which he didn't need particularly to defend. Yet it was largely an accident that Bentham was attacking Blackstone at all, and the work makes more sense and gains more importance when it is seen as part of Bentham's overall interests and projects rather than just as an attack on Blackstone. The account just given of Blackstone must therefore now be balanced by an account of Bentham himself.

Bentham's father was a successful attorney and he himself had been destined from an early age for the study of law. He was educated at Oxford and, at the time he wrote the *Fragment*, was living in the Inns of Court in London and, at least nominally, still studying the law. Earlier he had daily attended the courts in Westminster Hall, watching the judges at work. He had been called to the bar in 1769. From this time, following a normal course, he should have been looking for briefs and starting to practise on his own account. However, as has been seen, he was highly dissatisfied with the current condition of the law. So instead of further study of how the law was, or instead of contributing further to the filth by putting it into practice, Bentham started to write about how the law ought to be. He started on the project that would last him the rest of his life, a rational jurisprudence, complete and constructed from first principles, with all ancillary and relevant matters also considered. This would lead him into a general philosophical account of the nature of law and government, constitutional theory, and the planning of many more particular or practical projects, be they prisons or states. In the 1770s, which is the decade of the *Fragment* and the notes quoted at the beginning, most of this lay ahead. Yet Bentham had already developed a general account of the nature of law, an account of how the law ought to be, an analysis of offences and punishments, and the idea of classifying the law according to rational principles.

Bentham's central concern, therefore, was not with how the law was but with how it ought to be. The relevant distinction needed here is the one which Bentham himself makes near the start of the Preface to the *Fragment*, the distinction between an *expositor* and a *censor*. Blackstone, as he says, is an expositor, giving an account of the law as it is. Bentham himself is a censor, giving an account of the law as it ought to be. In Bentham's words, 'The *Expositor*, therefore, is always the citizen of this or that particular country: the *Censor* is, or ought to be the citizen of the world' (8). So Bentham's central work was not tied to the law of any particular country. He was, to use a word he himself invented, an international figure. At this time he was international in doctrine or intention. Later on he was international also in reputation. He advised people in many countries. He wrote to the Greeks, the Spaniards, the Americans. He was elected an honorary citizen of the new French Republic. As Hazlitt put it, writing shortly before his death, Bentham's reputation grew in proportion to the distance one moved from his home in Westminster. So, although what Bentham said at all periods could be applied to the law of particular countries, neither in the 1770s nor later did Bentham need to harry a commentary on the laws of one particular country in the way he did Blackstone.

Yet Bentham did harry Blackstone, and at length. Partly this is to be explained by the fact that Blackstone was the most prominent feature on Bentham's own local landscape when Bentham was learning the law; partly also explained by a tendency Bentham had all his life to subject works he disagreed with to close and relentless criticism. However, the central explanation is much more local or accidental. Bentham suddenly needed money. He had a relatively affluent family behind him and he normally had modest requirements. He existed quite happily for extended periods in rudimentary surroundings, legal chambers, cottages, hovels. For most of his life, as long as he could write, he had few other requirements. However, in the middle of the 1770s he fell in love with a penniless girl. His father had as a matter of fact made a similar match himself. Yet by now he was sufficiently aware of his position to have forgotten the passions and indiscretions of youth and it was a match he could not support. So, lacking the financial backing of his family, Bentham needed to try and make some money of his own, fairly quickly. He had a friend, John Lind, with whom he had co-operated in writing political pamphlets and through whom he had met his present beloved. Lind had currently got the idea of writing a commentary on Blackstone. Blackstone obviously made money; this might well do so as well; and so the idea arose of Bentham joining the project.

The original idea was that the friends co-operated on this as they had on their earlier pamphlets, which were mainly written by Lind. Bentham moved in with Lind and his wife and started working on Lind's draft. However, he soon took the project over, writing a critical commentary on the whole of Blackstone's introductory sections, that is on such matters as common law, statute law, natural law, and interpretation. It was in the course of this that he arrived at the difficulty, described in the Preface, of how he was to accommodate Blackstone's thoughts on government in general. So arose the *Fragment*, designed to see off the digression; and Bentham always supposed that the larger work, from which it was torn, might one day be published under a title such as the *Commentary on the Commentaries*. This did in fact eventually happen, but only in the present century, long after Bentham's death. While he lived, only the *Fragment* of the larger work appeared. There was no reason to do more at the time. The money-making project vanished, as did its immediate cause, Polly Dunkley of Colchester. The love affair lost momentum, or collapsed in the face of practicalities.

So much for the accidents that attended the birth of the *Fragment*. In this case, Bentham had no reason to persist with the larger work from which it was fragmented. He ceased to need the money and in any case was reconciled with his father once the affair ended. Indeed the stir which the publication of the *Fragment* produced led his father for the first time to think that Jeremy might not be totally wasting his time in study when he could be accepting briefs. However, publishing parts or fragments, starting things without completing them, was something which persisted. The next major work he published after the *Fragment*, and probably his most famous one, is called an 'Introduction' (the *Introduction to the Principles of Morals and Legislation*). Again the title is accurate. Just as the *Fragment* is a fragment, so the *Introduction* is an introduction. Treated now as a self-standing book, it was written as the introduction to a much larger work which never appeared. After that Bentham tended more and more to compile great masses of manuscript which were hacked into published form by others. Completion was left to contemporary disciples or to editors working long after his death. Thanks to his editor, Etienne Dumont, much of his work appeared in French before it was translated back into English. Bentham was temperamentally more inclined to take on new projects than finish old ones, and in any case his main overall project kept sprouting new limbs which he felt had to be properly developed before publication. At least in the case of the early works, the *Fragment* and *Introduction*, we have works prepared for the press by Bentham himself. Even if the overall projects did not come to fruition, the parts which did appear were polished for the reader. Here we have the works of the master himself; and by Bentham standards the *Fragment* is balanced, finished, highly readable.

This is one reason for taking the *Fragment* seriously. There is a much deeper reason, however. In spite of the indirections, the central thought on which Bentham was working all his life here makes its first, and extremely pithy, appearance. The shape of the work may be as a commentary on Blackstone, with all the accidents and indirections just described. However, the commentary has rifts, and these rifts are all loaded with Benthamite ore. Needing something to use against Blackstone, Bentham uses his own substantive thought; and his profound and original ideas keep squeezing themselves into footnotes. Indeed the footnotes are frequently as important as the main text and the rest of this *Introduction* will be devoted to displaying this by bringing out the central features of Bentham's main thought as they appear in the following text.

The chief aim of this thought is to construct an account of law and government from independent rational principles, as opposed to relying on the particular local traditions of authority which a group or country might happen to possess. Lawyers, that 'passive and enervate race' are to be criticised, criticised because they are 'deaf to the voice of reason and public utility' (13). It is reason which sets the independent standard of criticism, and reason is identified with utility. The word 'utility' is used because of Hume, whom Bentham credits (on page 51) with showing that the 'foundations of all *virtue* are laid in *utility*'. However, 'utility', 'happiness', 'pleasure', 'felicity' are all used interchangeably by Bentham. The principle of utility is hence none other than the fundamental axiom declared at the start of the work, namely that it is the greatest happiness of the greatest number that is the measure of right and wrong. As he points out in a footnote added to the second edition (on page 58), the principle of utility might better be called the greatest felicity principle or the greatest happiness principle.

So utility (happiness) is to be taken as the end, as the guide of right action. Bentham is thus an example, a prime or infamous example, of the evaluative doctrine known as utilitarianism. However, as the reference to Hume shows, Bentham neither invented utilitarianism nor thought that he had invented it. Between Hume and Bentham came Beccaria and Helvetius, other thinkers with the same general plan of advancing a new or rational science of law and politics. They are also mentioned by Bentham in the *Fragment*. Indeed the famous formula of the 'fundamental axiom', twice already quoted, appears word for word in the English translation of Beccaria (in the original it is 'la massima felicita divisa nel maggior numero'). So it is not the invention of utilitarianism for which Bentham is important. Rather, it is for showing in much greater detail than before how it might be applied.

A typical example of such an application is that made in the first chapter concerning the formation of government. It is natural, particularly for people like lawyers, to justify what happens in the present by what has happened in the past. So an attempt is made to justify present obedience to government by an account of its past formation. It is supposed that government arose out of an original agreement, or contract, in which the people contracted to obey a government in order to obtain its benefits. This is certainly the kind of justification which Bentham came across when he started his study of the law, as he describes in two pieces of autobiography printed here, the footnote to the present chapter entitled 'history of a mind perplexed by fiction' (51) and the later reminiscences reprinted in Appendix A. In the latter reminiscences, Bentham includes Blackstone among these lawyers. This is not completely fair. He is more accurate in the *Fragment* itself where he says that the original contract is 'by turns embraced and ridiculed by our Author' (51). Certainly Blackstone himself says (at times) quite clearly that there was no such thing. And this is the trouble. For most states and governments, very few people believe that there really was, as a specific historical event, an original contract either between the people themselves, or between the government and people.

Lawyers naturally believe in contracts, and even non-lawyers normally suppose that real contracts impose real obligations. However, this does depend on there actually being a contract. If, by contrast, the contract is supposed to be merely a fiction, then it would seem that the obligation imposed must also be merely fictional. This would, or should, be the end of the matter. Yet the problem that facts cited in justification were merely fictional would not by itself worry an eighteenth-century lawyer. The fiction of an original contract between people and government was merely one of the fictions which Bentham found running through the whole of the current law. Many of the central property cases were entirely fictional in character taking the form of an action between two men who did not exist, based on the fictional claim that one of these non-existent men had been ejected by the non-existent other. This was some of the filth which Bentham felt he had had to swallow on learning the law; and why his 'unpractised stomach revolted against their opiate' (52). It is why, in talking earlier about the lawyers, he says that the 'pestilential breath of Fiction poisons the sense of every instrument it comes near' (21). It is why, in the present case of the original contract and obedience to government, Bentham urged that 'the indestructible prerogatives of mankind have no need to be supported upon the sandy foundation of a fiction' (52).

However, even if the original contract were not fictional there would-still be problems. On this account, the obligation to obey the state depends on the obligation to honour contracts, and so can only be as valid as the latter obligation. Now, a contract can be looked at two ways, either as a legal or as a moral agreement. As a legal agreement, using contract as ultimate justification for obedience to the state is hopeless. As Bentham puts it in another place, 'contracts come from government, not government from contracts'; that is, the state must already be in play to support legal elements like contracts; hence these cannot be used to justify the state. So the obligation coming from contract in this case must be merely moral, being the obligation to keep a promise. The same historical difficulties apply as before. It is only if there was really a promise that there is any current obligation. No one is under any obligation to keep a promise which they might have made, or which it would have been rational for them to have made, but which was not made. Yet even if there really was a promise, the question remains why people should obey their promises. For Bentham it is because they are based on the principle of utility; it is only because keeping promises leads to an increase of happiness that people ought to obey them.

However, if utility is to be the ultimate justification of promise keeping, we might as well have started there in the first place without traversing this tortuous, and largely fictional, path through contracts, original contracts, non-existent agreements. This is Bentham's central message, and his chief concern, in the first chapter. We then get a clear justification of obedience to the state. The state is to be obeyed because it does good, that is, produces happiness. Justification is forward looking rather than backward looking, based on future happiness rather than past myth. The prerogatives of mankind are no longer founded on sand. Instead, the thing becomes a matter of calculation. It is a matter of finding whether the *'probable mischiefs of obedience are less than the probable mischiefs of resistance'* (56). So the justification of when to obey is also the justification of when not to obey, that is an explanation also of justified rebellion. To decide, the utilitarian must weigh the happiness which would come from obedience (considering everyone involved) against the happiness which would come from disobedience (considering everyone involved).

In the intervening centuries utilitarianism has run into many objections. J. S. Mill, who grew up under Bentham's influence, wrote his well-known work called *Utilitarianism* in an attempt to meet some of these, but utilitarianism is still the ethical theory which people love to hate. Some of the objections, however, are based upon misunderstanding, which, at least as it applies to Bentham, should now be removed.

Utilitarianism has been thought to be crass and insensitive as a system of personal ethics, unaware of the higher feelings. Some of this impression is due to Mill himself. In an earlier more rebellious phase, he wrote a famous essay about Bentham in which he singles out for disagreement a remark of Bentham's that, quantity of pleasure being equal, pushpin was as good as poetry. The origin of the phrase, now inexorably attached to Bentham because of Mill, is very obscure. It comes from manuscript which Bentham wrote in Russia in the decade after writing the *Fragment*, manuscript which, in the way described above, was first put into French by his French-speaking editor, Dumont, and only appeared in England, retranslated back into English, some forty years later by another editor, in a work called *The Rationale of Reward*. The point, however, was that in this, as in nearly all the rest of his work, Bentham was concerned with what the law should be, that is with what the government should do. He means that the legislature, considering what sort of subsidy (reward) should be granted to activities, should only consider the happiness which they bring the people. The modern equivalent would be the claim that opera would only qualify for state subsidy if it made people more happy than football. This, of course, is contentious. However, it is nothing like as contentious as the suggestion that people would be as fulfilled with pushpin as with poetry in their own personal lives. In his own personal life, Bentham preferred playing music to playing pushpin; and in any case, as Leigh Hunt remarked, he was the sort of person who could not even play badminton without wanting to stop and design a better shuttlecock. But this is not the point, either for Bentham or for his utilitarian predecessors. Utilitarianism is concerned with matters of state and government.

As a doctrine about government its point can be seen better when considering punishment rather than reward (although, in considering both, Bentham was typically both ahead of his time and complete in his treatment). Utilitarianism naturally develops principles of punishment, and it was these principles on which Bentham was centrally working in the decade in which he wrote the *Fragment*. People are to be taken as they are, desiring their own pleasure. The function of the state is to make these self-interested people do what they ought to do, as decreed in the fundamental axiom, that is do those things which lead to the happiness of the greatest number. Punishment places these two in step, artificially weighting certain courses of activity, so that self-interested people avoid them. In other words the punishment itself, being a pain, a lack of pleasure, is always an evil. It is, however, a justified evil if it leads to the greatest overall balance of pleasure. This will happen if the threat of punishment, or its actual infliction on a few people, makes people generally avoid those activities (like murder, rape, and theft) which cause general unhappiness.

The utilitarian theory of punishment is hence a deterrent theory. People are punished for future effect, rather than because of something that happened in the past. In the same way it was seen that obligations like keeping promises or obedience to the state were to be seen in future-directed terms; they did not arise because of some particular past event but becuase they would on balance lead to the greatest future overall happiness. In this way Bentham thought that he had substituted a clear course of action for an obscure one, and thought that he had substituted the path of plain reason, open equally to all people in all countries and at all times, for historical accidents of justification, open only to people in a particular country or at a particular time.

The objection to this would be that Bentham just takes his preferred goal of utility, gives it an honourable name by calling it the path of reason, and then just deploys it in the same way in which his opponents deployed their own favourite talisman, original contract, natural law, or whatever. In principle, it could be objected, they are the same; all justification has to start somewhere and Bentham just starts his justification in a different place, neither better nor worse than his opponents. However, Bentham thought that he had more on his side than a different, arbitrary, starting point; and to see this we must explore some of the other assumptions on which the theory of utilitarianism was based, as they are exposed in the *Fragment*.

The key word used in the above exposition was in fact clarity rather than reason. Bentham is above all concerned to appeal to the understanding, to make things certain, clear, obvious, where before they had been uncertain, confused, obscure. Blackstone is above all criticised because it is not clear what he is saying. It is not so much that Bentham objects to what he says but that he cannot make out what he means. So the approved accounts are going to be those that are clear and comprehensible. This applies whether it is an evaluative account or a descriptive one. Bentham just assumes that a comprehensible account is superior to a confused one, and that between the two there can be no neutrality or parity of esteem. Bentham was part of that eighteenth-century movement known as the enlightenment. The people he took himself to be following – Helvetius, Beccaria, Voltaire, Hume – were people who, originally inspired by Locke, wished to substitute clear thought for prejudice, enlighten minds, and remove medieval rubbish or confusion. It is in this spirit in which Bentham writes that Beccaria was 'the father of *Censorial Jurisprudence*. Montesquieu's work was of the mixed kind. Before Montesquieu all was unmixed barbarism' (14). Instead of the barbaric gothic tribes in the forest, we have the clearly lit cities of civilisation. However, as well as this general invocation of clarity, it is more useful (and more in the spirit of the enlightenment itself) to be specific. The key notion in understanding is meaning; and so the key particular task is to clarify the meaning of what is said. Once meaning is clarified, enlightenment follows.

This is why Bentham writes, in the lively manuscript passage about Blackstone reprinted in Appendix B, that 'To purge the science of the poison introduced into it by him and those who write as he does, I know but of one remedy; and that is by *Definition*, perpetual and regular definition, the grand prescription of those great physicians of the mind, Helvetius and before him Locke' (123). This much Bentham is just taking out of the enlightenment air (and notice the people he mentions). However, when thinking about how meaning could be clarified, Bentham became independently interesting. For he realised that definition alone would not be enough. One term could not be understood in terms of another, unless it was possible for some terms to be independently understood. In the tradition which Bentham belonged to, inspired by Locke, this meant: unless they related directly to someone's experience. In Locke this led to the distinction between simple and complex ideas; complex ideas can be analysed into simple ones, and simple ones are to be understood because they are directly experienced. Hume followed Locke directly in this; for example simple ideas like 'red' make no sense to someone without colour vision, yet we can analyse a complex idea like 'golden mountain' (Hume's example) into its simple parts. The analysis reveals the sense; and it has sense even though no one has seen a golden mountain. This is because they have separately seen golden things and mountains.

Locke thought that this sort of technique could be applied to the particular sort of complex ideas which he called 'mixed modes', taking as examples such as ideas as that of obligation or a lie. However, it was for just these kind of things that Bentham realised that the technique would not work. We presumably want 'obligation' to have sense; at least we do not normally think that all talk of obligations is meaningless rubbish. However, *obligation* cannot be broken down into its simple, directly experienced, parts in the way in which *golden mountain* can. For these Bentham therefore developed a special technique of his own. Realising that the primary unit of significance was the sentence rather than the word (or term), he thought that sense could be given to such terms by placing them in sentences which could then be analysed into, or replaced by, sentences in which the terms did not appear, and which referred in contrast to things which could be directly experienced. This Bentham referred to as his doctrine of *paraphrasis* and it is explained in the long and important footnote on page 108.

As Bentham says in the footnote, the method is particularly suited for Locke's mixed modes, and indeed he elsewhere gives an extended analysis of one of Locke's own examples, obligation. In the present work it is not obligation but the closely related notion of duty which is analysed. Just before Bentham gives his account of paraphrasis he explains both rights and duties; someone is said to have a right if someone else is under a duty towards him; and someone is under a duty to do something if he is liable, according to the law, to be punished for not doing it. So 'without the notion of punishment . . . no notion can we have of either *right* or *duty*' (108). We have an analysis in which right and duty are made sense of in terms of punishment, and punishment is made sense of in terms of pain threatened from a particular source. Paraphrasis is used because, instead of these notions like right and duty being taken to represent simple ideas which can be directly perceived and made sense of on their own, they are only made sense of in terms of sentences. Hence to talk of a right, for example a right of way, we take a sentence such as that John has a right of way over my land. We then make sense of, or analyse, it in terms of another sentence referring to duties, namely that I am under a duty to John not to impede his movement over my land. This in turn is made sense of in a further sentence saying that there is a law against impeding John, which can be analysed as that anyone impeding John is threatened with punishment (pain). The source of the threat can in turn be identified as that to which there is a habit of obedience in a particular country; habit, another of those weasel words which seem to refer to the imperceptible, can itself be analysed, as it is in a footnote to the first chapter (40). The whole account, therefore, appears in a series of linked footnotes, to the first and fifth chapters. This is why it was said above that the footnotes are often as important as the text.

Putting all this together, we find that we eventually come to pleasures and pains, which are objects of direct experience. Rights are analysed in terms of duties, and duties in terms of sanctions, that is the threat of pain. So all these abstract or obscure entities can be understood in terms of the directly experienced elements, pleasure and pain. Getting to them we get clarification; instead of all the windy, muddled, obscure, and misleading terms used by lawyers we have simple and palpable pleasure and pain ('and *pain* and *pleasure* at least, are words which a man has no need, we may hope, to go to a Lawyer to know the meaning of' (28)). So in this way we reach clarification, enlightenment, understanding. However, notice that it is a clarification which applies both to the fundamental evaluative vocabulary which Bentham uses in his account of the law and also to his fundamental descriptive vocabulary. Whether analysing the lawyer's basic vocabulary, of rights, duties, or such like, or whether deploying his basic critical vocabulary using the fundamental axiom of the principle of utility, in both cases we come down to pleasure and pain. If we ask what ought to be done we get the answer that pleasure should be maximised and pain minimised. If we ask what is meant by rights or obligations, we again get answers in terms of pleasure and pain. So pleasure and pain drive the whole machine; and it is the clarity that these words (which we do not need to consult lawyers about) are supposed to possess that gives the whole enterprise its illumination. This is why Bentham would have felt that someone could not be neutral between his ethical theory and another. As he put it elsewhere, 'when thus interpreted, the words *ought*, and *right* and *wrong*, and others of that stamp, have a meaning; when otherwise, they have none' (*Introduction*, chapter 1, section 12).

As well as these accounts of evaluation and of fundamental legal terms, we also have a Benthamite psychology. Again, it is in terms of pleasures and pains. Man is a pleasure-seeking animal and, more precisely than this, we can discover by observation the exact effects that differences in certainty, closeness, intensity, duration of pleasures and pains have on someone. All this is worked out in considerable detail in the next work, the *Introduction*. We have already seen how this applies to punishment. The principles are also applied in the later work in an analogous way to a great range of institutions. Bentham takes the fundamental principle declaring the evaluative end, and the basis assumption about human psychology, and then designs the institution so that people, following only their self-interest, do what they ought. This is the central principle in the design of Bentham's famous prison, the panopticon, as well as of his later design of constitutions. The central idea is very clearly laid out in the part of the proposed Introduction to the second edition of the *Fragment*, reprinted here as Appendix A. As can be seen on page 120, the central principles are first named separately and then put into co-operation; this Introduction was written at a time when Bentham was hard at work on consitutional theory.

It is one thing to design prisons or constitutions; it is another to get them put into effect. Bentham made a long, and ultimately unsuccessful, attempt to get his prison built. In the earlier parts of his life, when he wrote the *Fragment*, he thought that, in the spirit of the enlightenment, pointing out the confusions and showing how things could be better might be enough. It was supposed that men naturally wanted to be illuminated. Decades of struggle later, he realised that there were other forces at work; lawyers, the church, politicians (a collection which Bentham refers to at times as 'the Establishment') had an interest in keeping things as they were. They did not want to be persuaded. On being shown the new, clean, shiny truth, they shut their eyes. This led the older and more disillusioned Bentham into further insights of analysis, although it did not help with the central problem of how his proposals were to be put into effect. Some of the analysis can be seen in the proposed second edition Introduction printed here, which dates from the 1820s, that is from nearly fifty years after the first edition. As Bentham says, on page 116, where the 'Author of the *Fragment*' did not 'see the effect of any worse cause than inattention and prejudice' he now saw plainly 'the elaborately organized, and anxiously cherished and guarded products of sinister interest and artifice'.

However, the criticism of lawyers as a group, and the idea that such groups are moved by interest, was already there in the first edition. It is in the main text here that Bentham notes that 'interest smoothes the path to faith'; the attack on fictions, in the manuscript and to some extent in the text, shows awareness that the lawyers had an interest in maintaining their obscure practices. At all times he was fairly aware of the dimensions of the struggle. After all, someone wanting to use reason to clear away ancient rubbish must have some other source of power at his command to which the reason is to be attached; at any time it would be rather hopeful to suppose that merely pointing out something will lead someone to change his ways. Particularly when it is against his interest, an interest which the Benthamite psychology, early and late, insists that people follow. In the eighteenth century the philosophers wanting to change society appealed to the monarchs; in the nineteenth century they appealed to the people. Bentham followed both fashions at the appropriate times. In both cases the aim was the same, to put pressure on intermediate groups, such as lawyers or clerics, shored up with the authority of history. So Bentham first tried to appeal to such supposedly enlightened monarchs as Catherine the Great of Russia (this was one reason he was there writing about pushpin). In the next century the appeal was to the people, to democracy. This made better sense, on Bentham's own principles. For it could naturally be supposed that the greatest number had an interest in the greatest happiness of the greatest number. It was therefore in the interest of the effective power in a democracy, the majority, to be enlightened as to what ought to happen, that is about what would lead to the greatest happiness of the greatest number. The thought of the fundamental axiom in the work which follows, a work written in pre-revolutionary days in a world peopled by kings, leads inexorably to the democratic thought, the works written in favour of extended suffrage and secret ballot, of the later Bentham.

Principal events in Bentham's life

1748 Born, London (15 February).

1755 Westminster School, London.

1760 Queen's College, Oxford.

1763 Admitted to Lincoln's Inn; started to attend the law courts in London and Blackstone's lectures in Oxford.

1769 Admitted to the bar; at about this time starts to read Beccaria and Helvetius.

1774 Published translation with long preface of Voltaire's *Le Taureau blanc*.

1774 Falls in love with Mary (Polly) Dunkley; starts work with Lind on the *Comment*.

1776 *A Fragment on Government* published (April).

1780 Prints (apart from preface) the work which appeared as the *Introduction* in 1789.

1781 Commenced association with the political magnate, the Earl of Shelburne.

1785–8 In Russia. While in Russia wrote the *Defence of Usury* and *Panopticon Papers* and much of the manuscript used by Dumont in the 1802 edition.

1789 *Introduction to the Principles of Morals and Legislation* published. Also several occasional pamphlets designed for the new French revolutionary government; he also hoped that they would adopt his novel prison, the Panopticon, and a French translation was published.

1792 Made an honorary citizen of the French Republic. His father died; he came into some money and started trying to persuade the British government to build a panopticon which Bentham would manage as a private venture. A Bill to that effect passed the Lords in 1794, a site was purchased, but the negotiations were ultimately abortive.

1797–8 Wrote and published on poor law reform.

1799–1800 Worked on economics.

1802 Dumont's edition of Bentham published, the *traités de législation civile et pénale* (Paris). Bentham started work on evidence.

1809 First met James Mill (J. S. Mill's father), who worked as his secretary and supporter.

1811 Dumont published (in French) the material on reward and punishment. The panopticon project finally collapsed and Bentham was voted compensation by parliament. He started work on logic, language, classification.

1815 Published plan for a special school, the Chrestomathia.

1819 *Radical Reform Bill* published; an active supporter of the parliamentary reform movement.

1820s Much of the Bentham material produced by Dumont in French started to appear in English; in 1824 the specifically Benthamite, or utilitarian, journal, the *Westminster Review* was founded with Bentham's support.

1832 Death of Bentham.

Bibliographical note

General

Lyons, David *In the Interest of the Governed* Oxford University Press 1973

Parekh, Bhikhu (ed.) *Jeremy Bentham* Frank Cass 1974

Steintrager, James *Bentham* Allen & Unwin 1977

Hart, H. L. A. *Essays on Bentham* Oxford University Press 1982

Harrison, Ross *Bentham* Routledge & Kegan Paul 1983

Biography and intellectual background

Bentham *Memoirs and Correspondence* in (ed.) John Bowring *The Works of Jeremy Bentham* vols. X & XI 1843

Halévy, Elie *The Growth of Philosophic Radicalism* Faber & Faber 1928

Everett, C. W. *The Education of Jeremy Bentham* Columbia University Press 1931

Baumgardt, David *Bentham and the Ethics of Today* Princeton University Press 1962

Mack, Mary P. *Jeremy Bentham* Heinemann 1963

Long, Douglas G. *Bentham on Liberty* University of Toronto Press 1977

Writing on the *Fragment*, Blackstone, and law

Holdsworth, William *A History of English Law* vol. 13 1952 Methuen

Lyons, D. 'Rights, Claimants, and Beneficiaries' *Amer. Phil. Qtly* 6 (1969) 173–85

Raz, J. *The Concept of a Legal System* Oxford University Press 1970

Tarlton, Charles D. 'The Overlooked Strategy of Bentham's *Fragment on Government*' *Political Studies* 20 (1972) 397–406

Cross, R. 'Blackstone versus Bentham' *Law Qtly Rev.* 92 (1976) 516–27

Postema, G. J. 'The Expositor, the Censor, and the Common Law' *Canadian Jnl Phil.* 9 (1979) 643–70

Posner, Richard A. *The Economics of Justice* Harvard University Press 1981 Chapter 2

Postema, Gerald J. *Bentham and the Common Law Tradition* Oxford University Press 1986

Rights and utilities

Hart, H. L. A. 'Between Utility and Rights' in (ed.) Alan Ryan *The Idea of Freedom* Oxford University Press 1979

Waldron, Jeremy *Theories of Rights* Oxford University Press 1984

Sumner, L. W. 'Rights Denaturalised' in (ed.) R. G. Frey *Utility and Rights* Blackwell 1985

Fictions

Wisdom, John *Interpretation and Analysis in Relation to Bentham's Theory of Definition* Routledge & Kegan Paul 1931

Ogden, C. K. *Bentham's Theory of Fictions* Routledge & Kegan Paul 1932

Quine, W. V. O. 'Epistemology Naturalised' in *Ontological Relativity and Other Essays* Columbia University Press 1969

Quine, W. V. O. 'Five Milestones of Empiricism' in *Theories and Things* Harvard University Press 1981

Administration, panopticon

Poynter, J. R. *Society and Pauperism* Routledge & Kegan Paul 1968

Himmelfarb, Gertrude 'The Haunted House of Jeremy Bentham' in *Victorian Minds* Knopf 1968

Foucault, Michel *Discipline and Punish* Penguin 1977

Foucault, Michel 'The Eye of Power' in *Power/Knowledge* Harvester 1980

Bahmueller, Charles F. *The National Charity Company* University of California Press 1981

Hume, L. J. *Bentham and Bureaucracy* Cambridge University Press 1981

Evans, Robin *The Fabrication of Virtue* Cambridge University Press 1982

Politics and political economy

Robbins, Lionel *The Theory of Economic Policy in English Classical Political Economy* Macmillan 1952

Hutchison, T. W. 'Bentham as an Economist' *Econ. Jnl* 66 (1956) 288–306

Black, R. D. C. 'Jevons, Bentham, and De Morgan' *Economica* 39 (1972) 119–34

Rosenblum, Nancy *Bentham's Theory of the State* Harvard University Press 1978

Rosen, Frederick *Jeremy Bentham and Representative Democracy* Oxford University Press 1983

Writing by Bentham, and bibliography

Bentham's works are gradually being issued in the new *Collected Works* (originally Athlone University Press, now Oxford University Press); otherwise the unreliable nineteenth-century *Works* and editions have to be used. The *Correspondence* is practically complete in the new edition, and there are new editions of such central works as *An Introduction to the Principles of Morals and Legislation* (Athlone 1970) and *Of Laws in General* (Athlone 1970).

A fairly complete bibliography can be found in the *Bentham Newsletter* (Bentham Project, University College London).

Note on the text

All the Bentham text printed here has been taken from the volume in the new collected works edition of Bentham edited by J. H. Burns and H. L. A. Hart entitled *A Comment on the Commentaries and A Fragment on Government* (Athlone Press, London 1977). Bentham's text and his own notes are reprinted exactly as in that edition; the editorial footnotes of Burns and Hart are also reprinted, altered only so as to eliminate cross-reference to parts of that volume not reprinted here.

The text of the *Fragment* follows that of the first edition of 1776, although the two additions made in the second edition of 1823 are also given (and marked as such). The text was collated by Burns and Hart with the pirated Dublin edition of 1776, the second edition, the reprint in the nineteenth-century collected works edited by John Bowring, and with two later popular editions, F. C. Montague's of 1891 (OUP) and Wilfrid Harrison's of 1948 (Blackwell). Divergences are noted in footnotes (one curiosity picked up by the editors was that both the popular editions had followed the pirated Dublin edition rather than the official London one). The numbering of paragraphs is Bentham's own. In footnotes the abbreviation '*CW*' refers to the new collected works; 'Bowring' to the nineteenth-century collected works.

The Preface to the second edition was printed on paper matching the second edition but was not in the end published by Bentham, either as part of the second edition or separately. It first appeared, in a slightly altered form, in the nineteenth-century collected edition of Bentham edited by John Bowring (1838). Two sections of it are here reprinted from the Burns and Hart edition to form Appendix A.

Burns and Hart follow the original, with divergences from Bowring footnoted.

The Burns and Hart edition also printed some subsidiary manuscripts. One is a draft preface of Bentham's which gives a good expression of the general direction of his thoughts at the time when he was writing the *Comment* and the *Fragment*. A portion of it (pp. 346–50 of their edition) is reprinted here as Appendix B.

A

FRAGMENT

ON

GOVERNMENT;

BEING

An EXAMINATION of what is delivered,

On the Subject of GOVERNMENT in General

In the INTRODUCTION to

Sir *William Blackstone's* COMMENTARIES:

WITH A

PREFACE,

IN WHICH IS GIVEN

A CRITIQUE ON THE WORK AT LARGE.

Rien ne recule plus le progrès des connoissances, qu'un mauvais ouvrage d'un Auteur célèbre: parce qu'avant d'instruire, il faut commencer par détromper.

MONTESQUIEU Esprit des Loix, L. XXX. Ch. XV.

LONDON:

Printed for T. PAYNE, at the Mews-Gate; P. ELMSLY, opposite Southampton-Street in the Strand; and E. BROOKS, in Bell-Yard, Temple-Bar.

M.DCC.LXXVI.

Preface[1]

The age we live in is a busy age; in which knowledge is rapidly advancing towards perfection. In the natural world, in particular, every thing teems with discovery and with improvement. The most distant and recondite regions of the earth traversed and explored[2]— the all-vivifying and subtle element of the air so recently analyzed and made known to us[3]—are striking evidences, were all others wanting, of this pleasing truth.

Motives of the present undertaking

Correspondent to *discovery* and *improvement* in the natural world, is *reformation* in the moral; if that which seems a common notion be, indeed, a true one, that in the moral world there no longer remains any matter for *discovery*. Perhaps, however, this may not be the case: perhaps among such observations as would be best calculated to serve as grounds for reformation, are some which, being observations of matters of fact hitherto either incompletely noticed, or not at all would, when produced, appear capable of bearing the name of discoveries: with so little method and precision have the consequences of this fundamental axiom, *it is the greatest happiness of the greatest number that is the measure of right and wrong*, been as yet developped.[4]

---

[1] This Preface was written in the early months of 1776 and published in the first edition in April of that year. For the Preface written by Bentham for, but not published in, the second edition of 1823, cf. Appendix A, below.

[2] Bentham was writing in the period between Captain Cook's return in July 1775 from his second expedition and his departure, a year later, on his third, and had read John Hawkesworth's account, published in 1773, of the voyages to the southern hemisphere undertaken by Cook and others (cf. 71 below).

[3] Joseph Priestley's *Experiments and Observations on Different Kinds of Air* was published in three volumes between 1774 and 1777. For Bentham's keen interest in Priestley's work, see *Correspondence* (in *CW*), i and ii, as index.

[4] So spelt 1776: Dublin, and 1823, 'developed'.

3

Be this as it may, if there be room for making, and if there be use in publishing, *discoveries* in the *natural* world, surely there is not much less room for making, nor much less use in proposing, *reformation* in the *moral*. If it be a matter of importance and of use to us to be made acquainted with *distant* countries, surely it is not a matter of much less importance, nor of much less use to us, to be made better and better acquainted with the chief means of living happily in our *own*: If it be of importance and of use to us to know the principles of the element we breathe, surely it is not of much less importance nor of much less use to comprehend the principles, and endeavour at the improvement of those *laws*, by which alone we breathe it in security. If to this endeavour we should fancy any Author, especially any Author of great name, to *be*, and as far as could in such case be expected, to *avow himself* a determined and persevering enemy, what should we say of him? We should say that the interests of reformation, and through them the welfare of mankind, were inseparably connected with the downfall of his works: of a great part, at least, of the esteem and, influence, which these works might under whatever title have acquired.

Such an enemy it has been my misfortune (and not mine only) to see, or fancy at least I saw, in the Author of the celebrated COMMENTARIES *on the* LAWS *of* ENGLAND; an Author whose works have had beyond comparison a more extensive circulation, have obtained a greater share of esteem, of applause, and consequently of influence (and that by a title on many grounds so indisputable) than any other writer who on that subject has ever yet appeared.

History of it   It is on this account that I conceived, some time since, the design of pointing out some of what appeared to me the capital blemishes of that work, particularly this grand and fundamental one, the antipathy to reformation; or rather, indeed, of laying open and exposing the universal inaccuracy and confusion which seemed to my apprehension to pervade the whole. For, indeed, such an ungenerous antipathy seemed of itself enough to promise a general vein of obscure and crooked reasoning, from whence no clear and sterling knowledge could be derived; so intimate is the connexion between some of the gifts of the understanding, and some of the affections of the heart.

It is in this view then that I took in hand that part of the first volume to which the Author has given the name of INTRODUCTION. It is in this part of the work that is contained whatever comes under the denomi-

4

nation of *general principles*. It is in this part of the work that are contained such preliminary views as it seemed proper to him to give of certain objects real or imaginary, which he found connected with his subject LAW by identity of name: two or three sorts of LAWS of *Nature*, the *revealed* LAW, and a certain LAW of *Nations*. It is in this part of the work that he has touched upon several topics which relate to all laws or institutions[a] in general, or at least to whole classes of institutions without relating to any one more than to another.

To speak more particularly, it is in this part of his work that he has given a definition, such as it is, of that whole branch of law which he had taken for his subject; that branch, which some, considering it as a main stock, would term LAW without addition; and which he, to distinguish it from those others its *condivident branches*,[b] terms law *municipal*:—an account, such as it is, of the nature and origin of *Natural* Society the mother, and of *Political* Society the daughter, of Law *municipal*, duly begotten in the bed of Metaphor:—a division, such as it is, of *a* law, individually considered, into what he fancies to be its *parts*:—an account, such as it is, of the method to be taken for *interpreting* any law that may occur.

In regard to the Law of England in particular, it is here that he gives an account of the division of it into its two branches (branches, however, that are no ways distinct in the purport of them, when once established, but only in respect of the source from whence their establishment took its rise) the *Statute* or *Written* law, as it is called, and the *Common* or *Unwritten*:—an account of what are called *General Customs*, or institutions in force throughout the whole empire, or at least the whole nation;—of what are called *Particular Customs*, institutions of local extent established in particular districts; and of such *adopted* institutions of a general extent, as are parcel of what are called the *Civil* and the *Canon* laws; all three in the character of so many branches of what is called the *Common Law*:—in fine, a general account of *Equity*, that capricious and incomprehensible mistress of our fortunes, whose features neither our Author, nor perhaps any one is well able to delineate;—of *Equity*, who having in the beginning been

---

[a] I add here the word '*institutions*', for the sake of including rules of *Common* Law, as well as portions of *Statute* Law.
[b] *Membra condividentia.*—SAUND. Log. L. I. c. 46.[1]

---

[1] Robert Sanderson, *Logicae Artis Compendium*, 1618.

a rib of *Law*, but since in some dark age plucked from her side, when sleeping, by the hands not so much of God as of enterprizing Judges, now lords it over her parent sister:—

All this, I say, together with an account of the different districts of the empire over which different portions of the Law prevail, or over which the Law has different degrees of force, composes that part of our Author's work which he has styled the INTRODUCTION. His eloquent 'Discourse on the study of the Law', with which, as being a discourse of the rhetorical kind rather than of the didactic, I proposed not to intermeddle, prefaces the whole.

It would have been in vain to have thought of travelling over the whole of so vast a work. My design, therefore, was to take such a portion of it, as might afford a fair and adequate specimen of the character and complexion of the whole. For this purpose the part here marked out would, I thought, abundantly suffice. This, however narrow in extent, was the most conspicuous, the most characteristic part of our Author's work, and that which was most his own. The rest was little more than compilation. Pursuing my examination thus far, I should pursue it, I thought, as far as was necessary for my purpose: and I had little stomach to pursue a task at once so laborious and so invidious any farther. If *Hercules*, according to the old proverb, is to be known *ex pede*:[1] much more thought I, is he to be known *ex capite*.

In these views it was that I proceeded as far as the middle of the definition of the Law *municipal*. It was there I found, not without surprize, the digression which makes the subject of the present Essay. This threw me at first into no small perplexity. To give no account of it at all;—to pass wholly *sub silentio*, so large, and in itself so material a part of the work I was examining, would seem strange: at the same time I saw no possibility of entering into an examination of a passage so anomalous, without cutting in pieces the thread of the discourse. Under this doubt I determined at any rate, for the present, to pass it by; the rather as I could not perceive any connexion that it had with any thing that came before or after. I did so; and continuing my examination of the definition from which it digressed, I travelled on to the end of the Introduction. It then became necessary to come to some definitive resolution concerning this excentric part of it: and the result was, that being loth to leave the enterprize I had begun in this

---

[1] Plutarch, as reported by Aulus Gellius (*Noctes Atticae*, I.7), tells how Pythagoras deduced the stature of Hercules from the size of his foot.

respect, imperfect, I sat down to give what I intended should be a very slight and general survey of it. The farther, however, I proceeded in examining it, the more confused and unsatisfactory it appeared to me: and the greater difficulty I found in knowing what to make of it, the more words it cost me, I found, to say so. In this way, and by these means it was that the present Essay grew to the bulk in which the Reader sees it. When it was nearly completed, it occurred to me, that as the digression itself which I was examining was perfectly distinct from, and unconnected with the text from which it starts, so was, or so at least might be, the *critique* on that digression, from the *critique* on the text. The former was by much too large to be engrafted into the latter: and since if it accompanied it at all, it could only be in the shape of an Appendix, there seemed no reason why the same publication should include them both. To the former, therefore, as being the least, I determined to give that finish which I was able, and which I thought was necessary: and to publish it in this detached manner, as the first, if not the only part of a work, the principal and remaining part of which may possibly see the light some time or other, under some such title as that of '*A* COMMENT *on the* COMMENTARIES.'

In the mean time that I may stand more fully justified, or excused at least, in an enterprize to most perhaps so extraordinary, and to many doubtless so unacceptable, it may be of use to endeavour to state with some degree of precision, the grounds of that war which, for the interests of true science, and of liberal improvement, I think myself bound to wage against this work. I shall therefore proceed to mark out and distinguish those points of view in which it seems principally reprehensible, not forgetting those in which it seems still entitled to our approbation and applause.

There are two characters, one or other of which every man who finds any thing to say on the subject of Law, may be said to take upon him;—that of the *Expositor*, and that of the *Censor*. To the province of the *Expositor* it belongs to explain to us what, as he supposes, the Law *is*: to that of the *Censor*, to observe to us what he thinks it *ought to be.* The former, therefore, is principally occupied in stating, or in enquiring after *facts*:[c] the latter, in discussing *reasons.* The *Expositor*,

The business of the Censor *distinguished from that of the* Expositor

---

[c] In practice,[1] the question of *Law* has commonly been spoken of as opposed to that of *fact*: but this distinction is an accidental one. That a Law commanding or prohibiting

---

[1] I.e. in legal usage.

7

keeping within his sphere, has no concern with any other faculties of the mind than the *apprehension*, the *memory*, and the *judgment*: the latter, in virtue of those sentiments of pleasure or displeasure which he finds occasion to annex to the objects under his review, holds some intercourse with the *affections*. That which *is* Law, is, in different countries, widely different: while that which *ought to be*, is in all countries to a great degree the same. The *Expositor*, therefore, is always the citizen of this or that particular country: the *Censor* is, or ought to be the citizen of the world. To the *Expositor* it belongs to shew what the *Legislator* and his underworkman the *Judge* have done *already*: to the *Censor* it belongs to suggest what the *Legislator ought* to do *in future*. To the Censor, in short, it belongs to *teach* that *science*, which when by change of hands converted into an art, the LEGIS-LATOR *practises*.

The latter alone
our Author's

Let us now return to our Author. Of these two perfectly distinguishable functions, the latter alone is that which it fell necessarily within his province to discharge. His professed object was to explain to us what the Laws of England *were*. '*Ita lex scripta est*', was the only motto which he stood engaged to keep in view. The work of *censure* (for to this word, in default of any other, I find it necessary to give a *neutral* sense)[1] the work of *censure*, as it may be styled, or, in a certain sense, of *criticism*, was to him but a *parergon*—a work of supererogation: a work, indeed, which, if aptly executed, could not but be of great ornament to the principal one, and of great instruction as well as entertainment to the Reader, but from which our Author, as well as those that had gone before him on the same line, might, without being chargeable with any deficiency, have stood excused: a work which, when superadded to the principal, would lay the Author under additional obligations, and impose on him new duties: which, notwithstanding[2] whatever else it might differ in from the principal

such a *sort* of action, has been established, is as much a *fact*, as that an *individual* action of that sort has been committed. The establishment of a Law may be spoken of as a *fact*, at least for the purpose of distinguishing from any consideration that may be offered as a *reason* for such Law.

---

[1] *O.E.D.* entry seems to indicate that this neutral sense was archaic or obsolescent by the time Bentham wrote.

[2] Dublin, followed by Montague and Harrison, mistakenly inserts a comma at this point.

one, agrees with it in this, that it ought to be executed with impartiality, or not at all.

If, on the one hand, a hasty and undiscriminating condemner of what is established may expose himself to contempt; on the other hand, a bigotted[1] or corrupt defender of the works of power, becomes guilty, in a manner, of the abuses which he supports: the more so if, by oblique glances and sophistical glosses, he studies to guard from reproach, or recommend to favour, what he knows not how, and dares not attempt, to justify. To a man who contents himself with simply stating an institution as he thinks it *is*, no share, it is plain, can justly be attributed (nor would any one think of attributing to him any share) of whatever reproach, any more than of whatever applause the institution may be thought to merit. But if not content with this humbler function, he takes upon him to give *reasons* in behalf of it, reasons whether *made* or found by him, it is far otherwise. Every false and sophistical reason that he contributes to circulate, he himself is chargeable with: nor ought he to be holden guiltless even of such as, in a work where *fact* not *reason* is the question, he delivers as from other writers without censure. By officiously adopting them he makes them his own, though delivered under the names of the respective Authors: not much less than if delivered under his own. For the very idea of a *reason* betokens approbation: so that to deliver a remark under that character, and that without censure, is to adopt it. A man will scarcely, therefore, without some note of disapprobation, be the instrument of introducing, in the guise of a reason, an argument which he does not really wish to see approved. Some method or other he will take to wash his hands of it: some method or other he will take to let men see that what he means to be understood to do, is merely to report the judgment of another, not to pass one of his own. Upon that other then he will lay the blame; at least he will take care to repel it from himself. If he omits to do this, the most favourable cause that can be assigned to the omission is indifference: indifference to the public welfare—that indifference which is itself a crime.

It is wonderful how forward some have been to look upon it as a kind of presumption and ingratitude, and rebellion, and cruelty, and I know not what besides, not to allege only, nor to own, but to suffer any

Laws ought to be scrutinized with freedom

---

[1] So spelt 1776 and 1823: Dublin, followed by Montague and Harrison, 'bigoted'.

one so much as to imagine, that an old-established law could in any respect be a fit object of condemnation. Whether it has been a kind of *personification*, that has been the cause of this, as if the law were a living creature, or whether it has been the mechanical veneration for antiquity, or what other delusion of the fancy, I shall not here enquire. For my part, I know not for what good reason it is that the merit of justifying a law when right should have been thought greater, than that of censuring it when wrong. Under a government of Laws, what is the motto of a good citizen? *To obey punctually; to censure freely.*

Thus much is certain; that a system that is never to be censured, will never be improved: that if nothing is ever to be found fault with, nothing will ever be mended: and that a resolution to justify every thing at any rate, and to disapprove of nothing, is a resolution which, pursued in future, must stand as an effectual bar to all the *additional* happiness we can ever hope for; pursued hitherto would have robbed us of that share of happiness which we enjoy already.

Nor is a disposition to find 'every thing as it should be,'[1] less at variance with itself, than with reason and utility. The commonplace arguments in which it vents itself justify not what is established, in effect, any more than they condemn it: since whatever *now* is established, *once* was innovation.

Precipitate censure, cast on a political institution, does but recoil on the head of him who casts it. From such an attack it is not the institution itself, if well grounded, that can suffer. What a man says against it either makes impression or makes none. If none, it is just as if nothing had been said about the matter: if it *does* make an impression, it naturally calls up some one or other in defence. For if the institution is in truth a beneficial one to the community in general, it cannot but have given an interest in its preservation to a number of individuals. By their industry, then, the reasons on which it is grounded are brought to light: from the observation of which those who acquiesced in it before upon trust, now embrace it upon conviction. Censure, therefore, though ill-founded, has no other effect upon an institution than to bring it to that test, by which the value of those, indeed, on which prejudice alone has stamped a currency, is cried down, but by which the credit of those of sterling utility is confirmed.

[1] Cf. 18 below.

Nor is it by any means from passion and ill-humour, that censure, passed upon legal institutions, is apt to take its birth. When it is from passion and ill-humour that men speak, it is with *men* that they are in ill-humour, not with laws: it is men, not laws, that are the butt[1] of 'arrogance'.[d] Spleen and turbulence may indeed prompt men to quarrel with living individuals: but when they make complaint of the

[d] *'Arrogance'*; our Author calls it *the utmost arrogance*,* 'to censure what has, at least, a better chance to be right, than the singular notions of any particular man': meaning thereby certain ecclesiastical institutions. Vibrating, as it should seem, between passion and discretion, he has thought it necessary, indeed, to insert in the sentence that, which being inserted, turns it into nothing; After the word 'censure', 'with contempt' he adds, 'and rudeness': as if there needed a professor to inform us, that to treat any thing with contempt and rudeness is arrogance.[2] 'Indecency', he had already called it, 'to set up private judgment in opposition to public': and this without restriction, qualification, or reserve. This was in the first transport of a holy zeal, before discretion had come in to his assistance. This passage the Doctors *Priestly*[†] and *Furneaux*,[‡] who, in quality of Dissenting Ministers, and champions of dissenting opinions, saw themselves particularly attacked in it, have not suffered to pass unnoticed; any more than has the celebrated Author of the *'Remarks on the Acts of the 13th Parliament'*,[§] who found it adverse to his enterprize, for the same reason that it is hostile to every other liberal plan of political discussion.[4]

My edition of the Commentaries happens to be the first: since the above paragraph was written I have been directed to a later. In this later edition the passage about 'indecency' is, like the other about 'arrogance', explained away into nothing. What we are now told is, that 'to set up private judgment in (*virulent and factious*) opposition to public *authority*' (he might have added—or to *private* either) 'is indecency'. (See the 5th edit. 8vo. p. 50, as in the 1st.)[5] This we owe, I think, to Dr Furneaux. The Doctors Furneaux and Priestly, under whose well-applied correction our Author has smarted so severely, have a good deal to answer for: They have been the means of his adding a good deal of this kind of rhetorical lumber to the plentiful stock there was of it before. One passage, indeed, a passage deep-tinctured with religious gall, they have been the means

* IV Comm. p. 50.
† See Remarks, &c.
‡ See Letters to Mr Justice Blackstone, 1771. Second Edition.[3]
§ In the Preface.

---

[1] So spelt Dublin, Bowring, Montague, Harrison; 1776 and 1823, 'but'.
[2] The passage at IV Comm. 50 in fact reads 'Arrogance by treating with contempt and rudeness what has at least a better chance to be right...' etc.: the word 'censure' does not occur.
[3] Joseph Priestley, *Remarks on some paragraphs in the Fourth Volume of Dr Blackstone's Commentaries on the Laws of England, relating to the Dissenters*, 1769; Philip Furneaux, *Letters to the Honourable Mr Justice Blackstone, concerning ... Toleration ... and Religious Liberty...*, 1770.
[4] John Lind published the pamphlet in question in 1775. For Bentham's share in its composition see Bowring, x, 62–3; and Bentham to Samuel Bentham, 18 May 1775: *Correspondence* (in *CW*), i, 235.
[5] The insertion of the words 'virulent and factious' and 'authority' was made in the fourth edition (1770).

dead letter of the Law, the work of departed lawgivers, against whom no personal antipathy can have subsisted, it is always from the observation, or from the belief at least, of some real grievance. The Law is no man's enemy: the Law is no man's rival. Ask the clamorous and unruly multitude—it is never the Law itself that is in the wrong: it is always some wicked interpreter of the Law that has corrupted and abused it.^e

Thus destitute of foundations are the terrors, or pretended terrors, of those who shudder at the idea of a free censure of established institutions. So little does the peace of society require the aid of those lessons which teach men to accept of any thing as reason, and to yield the same abject and indiscriminating homage to the Laws here, which is paid to the despot elsewhere. The fruits of such tuition are visible enough in the character of that race of men who have always occupied too large a space in the circle of the profession: A passive and enervate

of clearing away entirely;* and in this at least, they have done good service.[1] They have made him sophisticate: they have made him even expunge: but all the Doctors in the world, I doubt, would not bring him to confession. See his answer to Dr Priestly.[2]

^e There is only one way in which censure, cast upon the Laws, has a greater tendency to do harm than good; and that is when it sets itself to contest their validity: I mean, when abandoning the question of expediency, it sets itself to contest the right. But this is an attack to which old-established Laws are not so liable. As this is the last though but too common resource of passion and ill-humour; and what men scarce think of betaking themselves to, unless irritated by personal competitions, it is that to which recent Laws are most exposed. I speak of what are called *written* Laws: for as to *unwritten* institutions, as there is no such thing as any certain symbol by which their authority is attested, their validity, how deeply rooted soever, is what we see challenged without remorse. A radical weakness, interwoven into the very constitution of *un*written Law.

* See Furneaux, Letter VII.

---

[1] The passage 'deep-tinctured with religious gall' removed in later editions ran in the first edition as follows (IV Comm. 52): 'As to the Papists their tenets are undoubtedly calculated for the introduction of all slavery both civil and religious: but it may with justice be questioned whether the spirit, the doctrines and the practice of the sectaries are better calculated to make men good subjects. One thing is obvious to observe that these have once within the compass of the last century effected the ruin of our church and monarchy; which the Papists have attempted indeed but have never yet been able to execute.'

In the seventh of his *Letters to the Honourable Mr Justice Blackstone*, Furneaux acknowledged that Blackstone had left out the offending passage in his latest edition, and described this as 'a degree of candour worthy not only of applause but of imitation'.

[2] In *A Reply to Dr Priestley's Remarks on the Fourth Volume of the Commentaries on the Laws of England* (1769), Blackstone denied that he had, as Priestley had supposed, censured thinking differently from the Church of England, claiming that he had censured only treating the church with contempt and rudeness and inveighing against its liturgy with bitterness and virulence.

race, ready to swallow any thing, and to acquiesce in any thing: with intellects incapable of distinguishing right from wrong, and with affections alike indifferent to either: insensible, short-sighted, obstinate: lethargic, yet liable to be driven into convulsions by false terrors: deaf to the voice of reason and public utility: obsequious only to the whisper of interest, and to the beck of power.

This head of mischief, perhaps, is no more than what may seem included under the former. For why is it an evil to a country that the minds of those who have the Law under their management should be thus enfeebled? It is because it finds them impotent to every enterprize of improvement.

Not that a race of lawyers and politicians of this enervate breed is much less dangerous to the duration of that share of felicity which the State possesses at any given period, than it is mortal to its chance of attaining to a greater. If the designs of a Minister are inimical to his country, what is the man of all others for him to make an instrument of or a dupe? Of all men, surely none so fit as that sort of man who is ever on his knees before the footstool of Authority, and who, when those *above* him, or *before* him, have pronounced, thinks it a crime to have an opinion of his own.

Those who duly consider upon what slight and trivial circumstances, even in the happiest times, the adoption or rejection of a Law so often turns; circumstances with which the utility of it has no imaginable connection—those who consider the desolate and abject state of the human intellect, during the periods in which so great a part of the still subsisting mass of institutions had their birth—those who consider the backwardness there is in most men, unless when spurred by personal interests or resentments, to run a-tilt against the Colossus of authority—those, I say, who give these considerations their due weight, will not be quite so zealous, perhaps, as our Author has been to terrify men from setting up what is now 'private judgment,' against what once was 'public':[f] nor to thunder down the harsh epithet of 'arrogance' on those, who, with whatever success, are occupied in bringing rude establishments to the test of polished reason. They will rather do what they can to cherish a disposition at once so useful and so rare:[g] which is so little connected with the

[f] See note (d) p. 11.
[g] One may well say *rare*. It is a matter of fact about which there can be no dispute. The truth of it may be seen in the multitude of *Expositors* which the Jurisprudence of every

causes that make popular discontentments dangerous, and which finds so little aliment in those propensities that govern the multitude of men. They will not be for giving such a turn to their discourses as to bespeak the whole of a man's favour for the defenders of what is established: nor all his resentment for the assailants. They will acknowledge that if there be some institutions which it is 'arrogance' to attack, there may be others which it is effrontery to defend. TOURREIL[h] has defended torture: torture established by the 'public judgment' of so many enlightened nations. BECCARIA ('indecent' and 'arrogant' Beccaria!) has condemned it.[3] Of these two whose lot among men would one choose rather,—the Apologist's or the Censor's?

Our Author why attacked in the character of an Expositor Of a piece with the discernment which enables a man to perceive, and with the courage which enables him to avow, the defects of a system of institutions, is that accuracy of conception which enables him to give a clear account of it. No wonder then, in a treatise partly of the *expository* class, and partly of the *censorial*, that if the latter department is filled with imbecillity,[4] symptoms of kindred weakness should characterize the former.

The former department, however, of our Author's work, is what, on its own account merely, I should scarce have found myself

nation furnished, ere it afforded a single *Censor*. When Beccaria came, he was received by the intelligent as an Angel from heaven would be by the faithful. He may be styled the father of *Censorial Jurisprudence*. Montesquieu's was a work of the mixed kind. Before Montesquieu all was unmixed barbarism. Grotius and Puffendorf were to Censorial Jurisprudence what the Schoolmen were to Natural Philosophy.[1]

[h] A French Jurist of the last age, whose works had like celebrity, and in many respects much the same sort of merits as our Author's. He was known to most advantage by a translation of Demosthenes. He is now forgotten.[2]

---

[1] Cesare, Marchese Bonesana Beccaria (1738–94) published *Dei delitti e delle pene*, anonymously, in 1764. A French version, modified with Beccaria's sanction, by André Morellet followed in 1767, and an English translation in the same year. Montesquieu's *De l'esprit des lois* was published in 1748. Hugo Grotius (1583–1645), *De Jure Belli ac Pacis*, 1625; Samuel Puffendorf (1632–1694), *Elementa Jurisprudentiae Universalis*, 1661, and *De Jure Naturae et Gentium*, 1672.

[2] Jacques de Tourreil (1656–1714) discussed torture in his *Essais de jurisprudence*, Question XV: 'Si la torture est une bonne voie de découvrir la vérité (*Œuvres*, 1721, i, 105).

[3] For Beccaria's condemnation of torture see *Dei delitti e delle pene*, § xii (in most edns.), but § xvi in F. Venturi's critical edition of the Italian text (Turin, 1965), following an edition of 1766. The words 'indecent' and 'arrogant' refer to IV Comm. 50: cf. n. *d* above.

[4] So spelt 1776 (and Dublin); 1823, Bowring, and modern edns. 'imbecility'.

disposed to intermeddle with. The business of simple *exposition* is a harvest in which there seemed no likelihood of there being any want of labourers: and into which therefore I had little ambition to thrust my sickle.

At any rate, had I sat down to make a report of it in this character alone, it would have been with feelings very different from those of which I now am conscious, and in a tone very different from that which I perceive myself to have assumed. In determining what conduct to observe respecting it, I should have considered whether the taint of error seemed to confine itself to parts, or to diffuse itself through the whole. In the latter case, the least invidious, and considering the bulk of the work, the most beneficial course would have been to have taken no notice of it at all, but to have sat down and tried to give a better. If not the whole in general, but scattered positions only had appeared exceptionable, I should have sat down to rectify those positions with the same apathy with which they were advanced. To fall in an adverse way upon a work simply *expository*, if that were all there were of it, would have been alike ungenerous and unnecessary. In the involuntary errors of the *understanding* there can be little to excite, or at least to justify, resentment. That which alone, in a manner, calls for rigid censure, is the sinister bias of the *affections*. If then I may still continue to mention as separate, parts which in the work itself are so intimately, and, indeed, undistinguishably blended, it is the *censorial* part alone that has drawn from me that sort of animadversion I have been led to bestow indiscriminately on the whole. To lay open, and if possible supply, the imperfections of the *other*, is an operation that might indeed of itself do service; but that which I thought would do still more service, was the weakening the authority of *this*.

Under the sanction of a great name every string of words however unmeaning, every opinion however erroneous, will have a certain currency. Reputation adds weight to sentiments from whence no part of it arose, and which had they stood alone might have drawn nothing, perhaps, but contempt. Popular fame enters not into nice distinctions. Merit in one department of letters affords a natural, and in a manner irrecusable presumption of merit in another, especially if the two departments be such between which there is apparently a close alliance.

Wonderful, in particular, is that influence which is gained over young minds, by the man who on account of whatever class of merit is esteemed in the character of a *preceptor.* Those who have derived, or fancy themselves to have derived knowledge from what he knows, or appears to know, will naturally be for judging as he judges: for reasoning as he reasons; for approving as he approves; for condemning as he condemns. On these accounts it is, that when the general complexion of a work is unsound, it may be of use to point an attack against the whole of it without distinction, although such parts of it as are noxious as well as unsound be only scattered here and there.

On these considerations then it may be of use to shew, that the work before us, in spite of the merits which recommend it so powerfully to the imagination and to the ear, has no better title on one account than on another, to that influence which, were it to pass unnoticed, it might continue to exercise over the judgment.

The Introduction is the part to which, for reasons that have been already stated, it was always my intention to confine myself. It is but a part even of this Introduction that is the subject of the present Essay. What determined me to begin with this small part of it is, the facility I found in separating it from every thing that precedes or follows it. This is what will be more particularly spoken to in another place.[2]

It is not that this part is among those which seemed most open to animadversion. It is not that stronger traces are exhibited in this part than in another of that spirit in our Author which seems so hostile to Reformation, and to that Liberty which is Reformation's harbinger.

It is not here that he tramples on the right of private judgment, that basis of every thing that an Englishman holds dear.[j] It is not here, in particular, that he insults our understandings with nugatory reasons; stands forth the professed champion of religious intolerance; or openly sets his face against civil reformation.

It is not here, for example, he would persuade us, that a trader who occupies a booth at a fair is a *fool* for his pains; and on that account no fit object of the Law's protection.[k]

---

[i] See the ensuing Introduction.   [j] See note [d].[1]

[k] 'Burglary',[*] says our Author, 'cannot be committed in a tent or a booth erected in a

[*] IV Comm. Ch. XVI. p. 226.[2]

---

[1] All the early edns., followed by Montague and Harrison, here insert a reference to note a; but this must be mistaken, since Bentham clearly intended another reference to his comments on IV Comm. 50 in note d.

[2] Bentham has modified the opening words to suit his context, slightly changed the punctuation, and omitted 'or' between 'market' and 'fair'.

16

It is not here that he gives the presence of *one* man at the *making* of a Law, as a *reason* why *ten thousand* others that are to *obey* it, need know nothing of the matter.[1]

It is not here, that after telling us, in express terms, there must be an 'actual breaking' to make burglary, he tells us, in the same breath, and in terms equally express, where burglary may be *without* actual breaking; and this *because* 'the Law will not suffer itself to be trifled with.'[m]

Reprehensible passages from the work at large

market fair; though the owner may lodge therein: *for* the Law regards thus highly nothing but permanent edifices; a house, or church; the wall, or gate of a town; and it is the *folly* of the owner to lodge in so fragile a tenement.' To save himself from this charge of folly, it is not altogether clear which of two things the trader ought to do: quit his business and not go to the fair at all: or leave his goods without any body to take care of them.

[*l*] Speaking of an Act of Parliament,* 'There needs', he says, 'no formal promulgation to give it the force of a Law, as was necessary by the Civil Law with regard to the Emperor's Edicts: *because* every man in England is, *in judgment of Law*, party to the making of an Act of Parliament, being present thereat *by his representatives*.' This, for aught I know, may be good *judgment of Law*; because any thing may be called judgment of Law, that comes from a Lawyer, who has got a name: it seems, however, not much like any thing that can be called *judgment of common sense*. This notable piece of *astutia* was originally, I believe, judgment of Lord Coke. It from thence became judgment of our Author: and may have been judgment of more Lawyers than I know of before and since.[2] What grieves me is, to find many men of the best affections to a cause which needs no sophistry, bewildered and bewildering others with the like jargon.

[*m*] His words are,† '*There must be an actual breaking*, not a mere legal *clausum fregit* (by leaping over invisible ideal boundaries, which may constitute a civil trespass) but a *substantial* and *forcible irruption*.' In the next sentence but two he goes on, and says,— 'But to come down a chimney *is* held a burglarious entry; for that is as much closed as the nature of things will permit. So also to knock at a door, and upon opening it to rush in with a felonious intent; or under pretence of taking lodgings, to fall upon the landlord and rob him; or to procure a constable to gain admittance, in order to search for traitors, and then to bind the constable and rob the house; *all these entries have been adjudged burglarious, though there was no actual breaking: for* the Law will not suffer itself to be trifled with by such evasions.' ... Can it be more egregiously trifled with than by such *reasons?*

I must own I have been ready to grow out of conceit with these useful little particles, *for, because, since*, and others of that fraternity, from seeing the drudgery they are continually put to in these Commentaries. The appearance of any of them is a sort of warning to me to prepare for some tautology, or some absurdity: for the same thing dished up over again in the shape of a reason for itself: or for a reason which, if a distinct one, is of the same stamp as those we have just seen. Other instances of the like hard treatment given to these poor particles will come under observation in the body of this

*I Comm. Ch. II. p. 178.[2]
†IV Comm. Ch. XVI. p. 226.

---

[1] The reference should be I Comm. 185.
[2] Coke, *Institutes*, IV, 26, cites on this point Sir Robert Thorpe, Chief Justice, without however giving the relevant Yearbook reference to 39 Edw. III (1365).

It is not here, that after relating the Laws by which peaceable Christians are made punishable for worshipping God according to their consciences, he pronounces with equal peremptoriness and complacency, that every thing, yes, 'every thing is as it should be.'[n]

It is not here, that he commands us to believe, and that on pain of forfeiting all pretensions to either 'sense or probity,' that the system of our jurisprudence is, in the whole and every part of it, the very quintessence of perfection.[o]

Essay. As to reasons of the first-mentioned class, of them one might pick out enough to fill a volume.

[n] 'In what I have now said', says he,* 'I would not be understood to derogate from the rights of the national Church, or to favour a loose latitude of propagating any crude undigested sentiments in religious matters. Of *Propagating*, I say; for the bare entertaining them, without an endeavour to diffuse them, seems *hardly* cognizable by any human authority. I only mean to illustrate the excellence of our present establishment, by looking back to former times. *Every thing is now as it should be*: unless, perhaps, that heresy ought to be more strictly defined, and no prosecution permitted, even in the Ecclesiastical Courts, till the tenets in question are by proper authority previously declared to be heretical. Under these restrictions it seems *necessary* for the support of the national religion', (the national religion being such, we are to understand, as would not be able to support itself were any one at liberty to make objections to it) 'that the officers of the Church should have power to censure heretics, but not to exterminate or destroy them.'

☞Upon looking into a later edition (the fifth) I find this passage has undergone a modification. After '*Every thing is now as it should be*', is added, '*with respect to the spiritual cognizance, and spiritual punishment of heresy.*' After '*the officers of the Church should have power to censure heretics,*' is added, '*but not to harass them with temporal penalties, much less to exterminate or destroy them.*'[1]

How far the mischievousness of the original text has been cured by this amendment, may be seen from Dr Furneaux, Lett. II. p. 30, 2nd edit.[2]

[o] I Comm. 140. I would not be altogether positive, how far it was he meant this persuasion should extend itself in point of time: whether to those institutions only that happened to be in force at the individual instant of his writing: or whether to such opposite institutions also as, within any given distance of time from that instant, either *had* been in force, or were *about* to be.

His words are as follows: 'All these rights and liberties it is our birthright to enjoy entire; unless where the Laws of our country have laid them under necessary restraints. Restraints in themselves so gentle and moderate, as will appear upon further enquiry, that no man of *sense* or *probity* would wish to see them slackened. For *all* of us have it in

* IV Comm. Ch. IV. p. 49.

---

[1] These changes were made in the fourth edition (1770).
[2] The second of Furneaux's *Letters to the Honourable Mr Justice Blackstone* was directed wholly against what he had taken to be Blackstone's original view: namely, that temporal penalties, as distinct from the mere censure of the church, might be used to suppress heresy. He acknowledged that Blackstone had intended to disclaim this in his later amendments, but complained that these did not do so with sufficient clarity.

It is not here that he assures us in point of fact, that there never *has* been an alteration made in the Law that men have not afterwards found reason to regret.[p]

our choice to do *every thing* that a good man would desire to do; and are restrained from nothing, but what would be pernicious either to ourselves or our fellow citizens.'

If the Reader would know what these rights and liberties are, I answer him out of the same page, they are those, 'in opposition to one or other of which *every* species of compulsive tyranny and oppression must act, having no other object upon which it can *possibly* be employed.' The liberty, for example, of worshipping God without being obliged to declare a belief in the XXXIX Articles, is a liberty that no '*good man*,'— no man of sense or probity,' 'would wish' for [1]

[p] I Comm. 70. If no reason can be found for an institution, we are to *suppose* one: and it is upon the strength of this supposed one we are to cry it up as reasonable; It is thus that the Law *is justified of her children.*[2]

The words are—'Not that the particular reason of every rule in the Law can, at this distance of time, be always precisely assigned; but it is sufficient that there be nothing in the rule *flatly* contradictory to reason, and then the Law will *presume* it to be well founded. And it hath been an ancient observation in the Laws of England,' (he might with as good ground have added—*and in all other Laws*) 'That whenever a standing rule of Law, of which the reason, perhaps, could not be remembered or discerned, hath been [*wantonly*] broke in upon by *statutes* or *new resolutions*, the wisdom of the rule hath in the end appeared from the inconveniences that have followed the innovation.'[3]

When a sentiment is expressed, and whether from caution, or from confusion of ideas, a clause is put in by way of qualifying it that turns it into nothing, in this case if we would form a fair estimate of the tendency and probable effect of the whole passage, the way is, I take it, to consider it as if no such clause were there. Nor let this seem strange. Taking the qualification into the account, the sentiment would make no impression on the mind at all: if it makes any, the qualification is dropped, and the mind is affected in the same manner nearly as it would be were the sentiment to stand unqualified.

This, I think, we may conclude to be the case with the passage above mentioned. The word '*wantonly*' is, in pursuance of our Author's standing policy, put in by way of salvo. *With* it the sentiment is as much as comes to nothing. *Without* it, it would be extravagant. Yet in this extravagant form it is, probably, if in any, that it passes upon the Reader.

The pleasant part of the contrivance is, the mentioning of '*Statutes*' and 'Resolutions' (Resolutions to wit, that is Decisions, of Courts of Justice) in the same breath; as if whether it were by the one of them or the other that a rule of Law was broke in upon, made no difference. By a *Resolution* indeed, a *new* Resolution, to break in upon a *standing* rule, is a practice that in good truth is big with mischief. But this mischief on what does it depend? Upon the rule's being a *reasonable* one? By no means: but upon its being a *standing*, an established one. Reasonable or not reasonable, is what makes comparatively but a trifling difference.

A new resolution made in the teeth of an old established rule is mischievous—on what account? In that it puts men's expectations universally to a fault, and shakes

[1] Bentham's reference at the beginning of this footnote is mistaken: the passage is at I Comm. 144.
[2] Matthew 11:19; Luke 7:35.
[3] I Comm. 70 has 'broken' for 'broke'. The square brackets round '*wantonly*' are Bentham's device for drawing attention to the word he comments on later in the note.

It is not here that he turns the Law into a Castle,[1] for the purpose of opposing every idea of 'fundamental' reparation.[q]

It is not here that he turns with scorn upon those beneficent

whatever confidence they may have in the stability of any rules of Law, reasonable or not reasonable: that stability on which every thing that is valuable to a man depends. Beneficial be it in ever so high a degree to the party in whose favour it is made, the benefit it is of to *him* can never be so great as to outweigh the mischief it is of to the community at large. Make the best of it, it is general evil for the sake of partial good. It is what Lord Bacon calls setting the whole house on fire, in order to roast one man's eggs.[2]

Here then the *salvo* is not wanted: a 'new resolution can never be acknowledged to be contrary to a standing rule,' but it must on that very account be acknowledged to be '*wanton*.' Let such a resolution be made, and 'inconveniences' in abundance will sure enough ensue: and then will appear—what? not by any means 'the wisdom of the rule,' but, what is a very different thing, the folly of breaking in upon it.

It were almost superfluous to remark, that nothing of all this applies in general to a statute: though particular Statutes may be conceived that would thwart the course of expectation, and by that means produce mischief in the same way in which it is produced by irregular resolutions. A new statute, it is manifest, cannot, unless it be simply a declaratory one, be made in any case, but it must break in upon some standing rule of Law. With regard to a Statute then to tell us that a 'wanton' one has produced 'inconveniences,' what is it but to tell us that a thing that has been mischievous has produced mischief?

Of this temper are the arguments of all those doating politicians, who, when out of humour with a particular innovation without being able to tell why, set themselves to declaim against *all* innovation, because it is innovation. It is the nature of owls to hate the light: and it is the nature of those politicians who are wise by rote, to detest every thing that forces them either to find (what, perhaps, is impossible) reasons for a favourite persuasion, or (what is not endurable) to discard it.

[q] III Comm. 268, at the end of Ch. XVII, which concludes with three pages against Reformation. Our Author had better, perhaps, on this occasion, have kept clear of allegories: he should have considered whether they might not be retorted on him with severe retaliation. He should have considered, that it is not easier to *him* to turn the Law into a Castle, than it is to the imaginations of impoverished suitors to people it with Harpies. He should have thought of the den of Cacus, to whose enfeebled optics, to whose habits of dark and secret rapine, nothing was so hateful, nothing so dangerous, as the light of day.[3]

---

[1] 'We inhabit an old Gothic castle, erected in the days of chivalry, but fitted up for a modern inhabitant. The moated ramparts, the embattled towers, and the trophied halls, are magnificent and venerable, but useless. The inferior apartments, now converted into rooms of convenience, are chearful and commodious, though their approaches are winding and difficult.' Blackstone is here (III Comm. 267–8) defending the 'intricacy of our legal process'.

[2] Bacon, Essay 23, 'Of Wisdom for a Man's Self': '...and certainly it is the nature of extreme self-lovers as they will set a house on fire and it were but to roast their eggs.'

[3] According to Roman legend, the monster Cacus lived in a cave on the Aventine hill and was killed by Hercules after stealing some of the cattle taken by the latter from Geryon.

Legislators, whose care it has been to pluck the mask of Mystery from the face of Jurisprudence.ʳ

ʳ III Comm. 322. It is from the decisions of Courts of Justice that those rules of Law are framed, on the knowledge of which depend the life, the fortune, the liberty of every man in the nation. Of these decisions the Records are, according to our Author (I Comm. 71) the most authentic histories. These Records were, till within these five-and-forty years, in Law-Latin: a language which, upon a high computation, about one man in a thousand used to fancy himself to understand. In this Law-Latin it is that our Author is satisfied they should have been continued, because the pyramids of Egypt have stood longer than the temples of Palmyra. He observes to us, that the Latin language could not express itself on the subject without borrowing a multitude of words from our own: which is to help to convince us that of the two the former is the fittest to be employed. He gives us to understand that, taking it altogether, there could be no room to complain of it, seeing it was not more unintelligible than the jargon of the schoolmen, some passages of which he instances; and then he goes on, 'This technical Latin continued in use from the time of its first introduction till the subversion of our ancient constitution under Cromwell; when, among many other innovations on the body of the Law, some for the better and some for the worse, the language of our Records was altered and turned into English. But at the Restoration of King Charles, this *novelty* was no longer countenanced; the practisers finding it very difficult to express themselves so concisely or significantly in any other language but the Latin. And thus it continued without any sensible inconvenience till about the year 1730, when it was again thought proper that the Proceedings at Law should be *done* into English, and it was accordingly so ordered by statute 4 Geo. II. c. 26.

'This was done (continues our Author) in order that the common people might have knowledge and understanding of what was alleged or done for and against them in the process and pleadings, the judgment and entries in a cause. Which purpose I know not how well it has answered; but am *apt to suspect* that the people are now, after many years' experience, *altogether* as ignorant in matters of law as before.'[1]

In this scornful passage the words *novelty*—*done* into English—*apt* to *suspect*—*altogether* as ignorant—sufficiently speak the affection of the mind that dictated it. It is thus that our Author chuckles over the supposed defeat of the Legislature with a fond exultation which all his discretion could not persuade him to suppress.

The case is this. A large portion of the body of the Law was, by the bigotry or the artifice of Lawyers, locked up in an illegible character, and in a foreign tongue. The statute he mentions obliged them to give up their hieroglyphics, and to restore the native language to its rights.

This was doing much; but it was not doing every thing. Fiction, tautology, technicality, circuity, irregularity, inconsistency remain. But above all the pestilential breath of Fiction poisons the sense of every instrument it comes near.

The consequence is, that the Law, and especially that part of it which comes under the topic of Procedure, *still* wants much of being generally intelligible. The fault then of the Legislature is their not having done *enough*. His quarrel with them is for having done any thing at all. In doing what they did, they set up a light, which, obscured by many remaining clouds, is still but too apt to prove an *ignis fatuus*: our Author, instead of calling for those clouds to be removed, deprecates all light, and pleads for total darkness.

---

[1] III Comm. 322 has 'antient' for 'ancient', and 'in the law' for 'on the body of the law'.

If here,[s] as every where, he is eager to hold the cup of flattery to high station, he has stopt short, however, in this place, of idolatry.[t]

Not content with representing the alteration as useless, he would persuade us to look upon it as mischievous. He speaks of 'inconveniences'. What these inconveniences are it is pleasant to observe.

In the first place, many young practisers, spoilt by the indulgence of being permitted to carry on their business in their mother-tongue, know not how to read a Record upon the old plan. 'Many Clerks and Attornies', says our Author, 'are hardly able to read, much less to understand a Record of so modern a date as the reign of George the First.'

What the mighty evil is here, that is to outweigh the mischief of almost universal ignorance, is not altogether clear: Whether it is, that certain Lawyers, in a case that happens very rarely, may be obliged to get assistance: or that the business in such a case may pass from those who do *not* understand it to those who do.

In the next place, he observes to us, 'it has much enhanced the expense of all legal proceedings: for since the practisers are confined (for the sake of the stamp-duties, which are thereby considerably increased) to write only a stated number of words in a sheet; and as the English language, through the multitude of its particles, is much more verbose than the Latin; it follows, that the number of sheets must be very much augmented by the change'.[1]

I would fain persuade myself, were it possible, that this unhappy sophism could have passed upon the inventor. The sum actually levied on the public on that score is, upon the whole, either a proper sum or it is not. If it *is*, why mention it as an evil? If it is *not*, what more obvious remedy than to set the duties lower?

After all, what seems to be the real evil, notwithstanding our Author's unwillingness to believe it, is, that by means of this alteration, men at large are in a somewhat better way of knowing what their Lawyers are about: and that a disinterested and enterprising Legislator, should happily such an one arise, would now with somewhat less difficulty be able to see before him.

[s] V. infra, Ch. III. par. 7. p. 464.
[t] In the Seventh Chapter of the First Book. The King has '*attributes*';[*] he possesses '*ubiquity*';[†] he is '*all-perfect* and *immortal*.'[‡]

These childish paradoxes, begotten upon servility by false wit, are not more adverse to manly sentiment, than to accurate apprehension. Far from contributing to place the institutions they are applied to in any clear point of view, they serve but to dazzle and confound, by giving to Reality the air of Fable. It is true, they are not altogether of our Author's invention: it is he, however, that has revived them, and that with improvements and additions.

One might be apt to suppose they were no more than so many transient flashes of ornament: it is quite otherwise. He dwells upon them in sober sadness. The attribute of '*ubiquity*,' in particular, he lays hold of, and makes it the basis of a chain of reasoning. He spins it out into consequences: he makes one thing '*follow*' from it, and another thing be so and so 'for the same *reason*:' and he uses emphatic terms, as if for fear he should not

[*] I Comm. 242.   [†] I Comm. Ch. VII. pp. 234, 238, 242. First Edition.
[‡] I Comm. Ch. VII. p. 260. First Edition.[2]

---

[1] III Comm. 322–3.
[2] Bentham's references in these notes are evidently mistaken. For the king's 'attributes' the reference should be I Comm. 241; his 'ubiquity' is not explicitly mentioned until I Comm. 270; and his 'absolute perfection' and 'absolute immortality' are dealt with respectively at I Comm. 246–8 and I Comm. 249.

It is not then, I say, *this* part, it is not even any part of that Introduction, to which alone I have any thoughts of extending my examination, that is the principal seat of that poison, against which it was the purpose of this attempt to give an antidote. The subject handled in this part of the work is such, as admits not of much to be said in the person of the Censor. Employed, as we have seen, in settling matters of a preliminary nature—in drawing outlines, it is not in this part that there was occasion to enter into the details of any particular institution. If I chose the Introduction then in preference to any other part, it was on account of its affording the fairest specimen of the whole, and not on account of its affording the greatest scope for censure.

Let us reverse the tablet. While with this freedom I expose our Author's ill deserts, let me not be backward in acknowledging and paying homage to his various merits: a justice due, not to him alone, but to that Public, which now for so many years has been dealing out to him (it cannot be supposed altogether without title) so large a measure of its applause. *Its merits*

Correct, elegant, unembarrassed, ornamented, the *style* is such, as could scarce fail to recommend a work still more vicious in point of *matter* to the multitude of readers.

He it is, in short, who first of all institutional writers, has taught Jurisprudence to speak the language of the Scholar and the Gentleman: put a polish upon that rugged science: cleansed her from the dust and cobwebs of the office: and if he has not enriched her with that precision that is drawn only from the sterling treasury of the

---

be thought to be in earnest. 'From the ubiquity', says our Author (1 Comm. p. 260)[1] 'it *follows*, that the King can never be nonsuit; *for* a nonsuit is the desertion of the suit or action by the non-appearance of the plaintiff in Court.'—'For the same reason also the King is not to appear by his Attorney, as other men do; for he always appears in contemplation of Law in his *own proper* person.'

This is the case so soon as you come to this last sentence of the paragraph. For so long as you are at the last but two, 'it is the regal office, and *not* the royal person, that is always present'. All this is so drily and so strictly true, that it serves as the groundwork of a metaphor that is brought in to embellish and enliven it. The King, we see, *is*, that is to say is *not*, present in Court. The King's Judges are present too. So far is plain downright truth. These Judges, then, speaking metaphorically, are so many looking-glasses, which have this singular property, that when a man looks at them, instead of seeing his own face in them, he sees the King's. 'His Judges', says our Author, 'are the mirror by which the King's image is reflected.'

---

[1] The correct reference is I Comm. 270.

sciences, has decked her out, however, to advantage, from the toilette of classic erudition: enlivened her with metaphors and allusions: and sent her abroad in some measure to instruct, and in still greater measure to entertain, the most miscellaneous and even the most fastidious societies.

The merit to which, as much perhaps as to any, the work stands indebted for its reputation, is the enchanting harmony of its numbers: a kind of merit that of itself is sufficient to give a certain degree of celebrity to a work devoid of every other. So much is man governed by the ear.

The function of the Expositor may be conceived to divide itself into two branches: that of *history*, and that of simple *demonstration*. The business of history is to represent the Law in the state it *has* been in, in past periods of its existence: the business of simple demonstration in the sense in which I will take leave to use the word, is to represent the Law in the state it *is* in for the time being.[u]

Again, to the head of demonstration belong the several businesses of *arrangement*, *narration* and *conjecture*. Matter of narration it may be called, where the Law is supposed to be explicit, clear, and settled: matter of conjecture or interpretation, where it is obscure, silent, or unsteady. It is matter of arrangement to *distribute* the several real or supposed institutions into different masses, for the purpose of a general survey; to determine the *order* in which those masses shall be brought to view; and to find for each of them a *name*.

The business of narration and interpretation are conversant chiefly about particular institutions. Into the details of particular institutions it has not been my purpose to descend. On these topics, then, I may say, in the language of procedure, *non sum informatus*. Viewing the

---

[u] The word *demonstration* may here seem, at first sight, to be out of place. It will be easily perceived that the sense here put upon it is not the same with that in which it is employed by Logicians and Mathematicians. In our own language, indeed, it is not very familiar in any other sense than theirs: but on the Continent it is currently employed in many other sciences. The French, for example, have their *demonstrateurs de botanique, d'anatomie, de physique experimentale, &c.* I use it out of necessity; not knowing of any other that will suit the purpose.[1]

---

[1] The word 'demonstration' is sometimes, though now rarely, used in the sense, not of proof, but of explanation and description. The word 'demonstrator' is of course now well established in precisely the sense indicated by Bentham for the French *démonstrateur*.

24

work in this light, I have nothing to add to or to except against the public voice.

History is a branch of instruction which our Author, though not rigidly necessary to his design, called in, not without judgment, to cast light and ornament on the dull work of simple *demonstration*: this part he has executed with an elegance which strikes every one: with what fidelity, having not very particularly examined, I will not take upon me to pronounce.

Among the most difficult and the most important of the functions of the *demonstrator* is the business of *arrangement*. In this our Author has been thought, and not, I conceive, without justice, to excel; at least in comparison of any thing in that way that has hitherto appeared. 'Tis to him we owe such an arrangement of the elements of Jurisprudence, as wants little, perhaps, of being the best that a technical nomenclature will admit of. A technical nomenclature, so long as it is admitted to mark out and denominate the principal heads, stands an invincible obstacle to every other than a technical arrangement. For to *denominate* in general terms, what is it but to arrange? and to arrange under heads, what is it but to *denominate* upon a large scale? A technical arrangement, governed then in this manner, by a technical nomenclature, can never be otherwise than *confused* and *unsatisfactory*. The reason will be sufficiently apparent, when we understand what sort of an arrangement that must be which can be properly termed a *natural* one.

That arrangement of the materials of any science may, I take it, be termed a *natural* one, which takes such properties to characterize them by, as men in general are, by the common constitution of man's *nature*, disposed to attend to: such, in other words, as *naturally*, that is readily, engage, and firmly fix the attention of any one to whom they are pointed out. The materials, or elements here in question, are such actions as are the objects of what we call Laws or Institutions. *Idea of a* natural *arrangement*

Now then, with respect to actions in general, there is no property in them that is calculated so readily to engage, and so firmly to fix the attention of an observer, as the *tendency* they may have *to*, or *divergency* (if one may so say)[1] *from*, that which may be styled the common *end* of

---

[1] It is not wholly clear why Bentham hesitated over this use of the term 'divergency', though *O.E.D.* does seem to indicate that its use in a figurative sense was a rather later development.

all of them. The end I mean is *Happiness*:^{v} and this *tendency* in any act is what we style its *utility*: as this *divergency* is that to which we give the name of *mischievousness*. With respect then to such actions in particular as are among the objects of the Law, to point out to a man the *utility* of them or the mischievousness, is the only way to make him see *clearly* that property of them which every man is in search of; the only way, in short, to give him *satisfaction*.

From *utility* then we may denominate a *principle*, that may serve to preside over and govern, as it were, such arrangement as shall be made of the several institutions or combinations of institutions that compose the matter of this science: and it is this principle, that by putting its stamp upon the several names given to those combinations, can alone render *satisfactory* and *clear* any arrangement that can be made of them.

Governed in this manner by a principle that is recognized by all men, the same arrangement that would serve for the jurisprudence of any one country, would serve with little variation for that of any other.

Yet more. The mischievousness of a bad Law would be detected, at least the utility of it would be rendered suspicious, by the difficulty of finding a place for it in such an arrangement: while, on the other hand, a *technical* arrangement is a sink that with equal facility will swallow any garbage that is thrown into it.

That this advantage may be possessed by a natural arrangement, is not difficult to conceive. Institutions would be characterized by it in the only universal way in which they can be characterized; by the nature of the several *modes* of *conduct* which, by prohibiting, they constitute *offences*^{w}.^{2}

---

^{v} Let this be taken for a truth upon the authority of *Aristotle*: I mean by those, who like the authority of Aristotle better than that of their own experience. Πᾶσα τέχνη, says that philosopher, καὶ πᾶσα μέθοδος· ὁμοίως δὲ πρᾶξίς τε καὶ προαίρεσις, ἀγαθοῦ τινὸς ἐφίεσθαι δοκεῖ· διὸ καλῶς ἀπεφήναντο τἀγαθόν, οὗ πάντα ἐφίεται. Διαφορὰ δέ τις φαίνεται τῶν (understand τοιούτων) ΤΕΛΩΝ.—Arist. Eth. ad Nic. L. I. c. 1.^{1}

^{w} Offences, the Reader will remember, may as well be offences of *omission* as of *commission*. I would avoid the embarrassment of making separate mention of such Laws as exert themselves in *commanding*. 'Tis on this account I use the phrase '*mode of conduct*,' which includes *omissions* or *forbearances*, as well as *acts*.

---

^{1} 'Every art and every investigation, and likewise every action and purpose seems to aim at some good: hence it has been well said that the Good is that at which all things aim. It is true that a certain variety is to be observed among the ends.' There seems to be no justification for Bentham's insertion of τοιούτων.

^{2} Bentham's vast classificatory scheme of offences constructed on the principles

These offences would be collected into classes denominated by the various modes of their *divergency* from the common *end*; that is, as we have said, by their various forms and degrees of *mischievousness*: in a word, by those properties which are *reasons* for their being made *offences*: and whether any such mode of conduct possesses any such property is a question of experience.[x] Now, a bad Law is that which prohibits a mode of conduct that is *not* mischievous.[y] Thus would it be found impracticable to place the mode of conduct prohibited by a bad law under any denomination of offence, without asserting such a matter of fact as is contradicted by experience. Thus cultivated, in short, the soil of Jurisprudence would be found to repel in a manner every evil institution; like that country which refuses, we are told, to harbour any thing venomous in its bosom.[1]

The *synopsis* of such an arrangement would at once be a compendium of *expository* and of *censorial* Jurisprudence: nor would it serve more effectually to instruct the *subject*, than it would to justify or reprove the *Legislator*.

Such a synopsis, in short, would be at once a map, and that an universal one, of Jurisprudence as it *is*, and a slight but comprehensive sketch of what it *ought to be*. For, the *reasons* of the several institutions comprised under it would stand expressed, we see, and that uniformly (as in our Author's synopsis they do in scattered instances) by the names given to the several classes under which those institutions are comprised. And what reasons? Not *technical* reasons, such as none but a Lawyer gives, nor any but a Lawyer would put up with;[z] but reasons, such as were they in themselves what they might

---

[x] See note e1, p. 29.   [y] See note *w*, p. 24.

[z] *Technical* reasons: so called from the Greek τέχνη, which signifies an art, science, or profession.

Utility is that standard to which men in general (except in here and there an instance where they are deterred by prejudices of the religious class, or hurried away by the force of what is called *sentiment* or *feeling*),[2] Utility, as we have said, is the standard to which they refer a Law or institution in judging of its title to approbation or

---

here expounded forms the lengthy Chapter XVI on the 'Division of Offences' in *An Introduction to the Principles of Morals and Legislation* (in *CW*, 187–280). There also he further discusses the merits of a 'natural' classification and arrangement (ibid., 272–4).

[1] A reference to the legend that St Patrick destroyed all snakes in Ireland.

[2] 1776, Dublin, and 1823 all have a full stop after the parenthesis, as does Montague. Bowring substitutes a dash, and Harrison a comma, one or other of which the sense requires.

and ought to be, and expressed too in the manner they might and ought to be, any man might see the force of as well as he.

Nor in this is there any thing that need surprize us. The consequences of any Law, or of any act which is made the object of a Law, the only consequences that men are at all interested in, what are they but *pain* and *pleasure*? By some such words then as *pain* and *pleasure*, they may be expressed: and *pain* and *pleasure* at least, are words which a man has no need, we may hope, to go to a Lawyer to know the meaning of.[a1] In the synopsis then of that sort of arrangement which alone deserves the name of a natural one, terms such as these, terms which if they can be said to belong to any science, belong rather to Ethics than to Jurisprudence, even than to universal Jurisprudence, will engross the most commanding stations.

What then is to be done with those names of classes that are purely technical?—With offences, for example, against prerogative, with misprisions, contempts, felonies, præmunires?[b1] What relation is it that these mark out between the Laws that concern the sorts of acts they are respectively put to signify, and that *common end* we have been speaking of? Not any. In a natural arrangement what then would become of them? They would either be banished at once to the region of *quiddities* and *substantial forms*; or if, and in deference to attachments too inveterate to be all at once dissolved, they were still to be indulged a place, they would be stationed in the corners and byeplaces of the Synopsis: stationed, not as now to *give* light, but to *receive* it. But more of this, perhaps, at some future time.

Merits of the work resumed

To return to our Author. Embarrassed, as a man must needs be, by this blind and intractable nomenclature, he will be found, I conceive, to have done as much as could reasonably be expected of a writer so

disapprobation. Men of Law, corrupted by interests, or seduced by illusions, which it is not here our business to display, have deviated from it much more frequently, and with much less reserve. Hence it is that such reasons as pass with Lawyers, and with no one else, have got the name of *technical* reasons; reasons peculiar to the *art*, peculiar to the profession.

[a1] The *reason* of a Law, in short, is no other than the *good* produced by the mode of conduct which it enjoins, or (which comes to the same thing) the *mischief* produced by the mode of conduct which it prohibits. This *mischief* or this *good*, if they be real, cannot but shew themselves somewhere or other in the shape of *pain* or *pleasure*.

[b1] See in the Synoptical Table prefixed to our Author's *Analysis*, the last page comprehending Book IV.[1]

---

[1] W. Blackstone, *An Analysis of the Laws of England* (1756). The present reference is to p. [xii] of the sixth edition, 1771.

circumstanced; and more and better than was ever done before by any one.

In one part, particularly, of his Synopsis,[c1] several fragments of a sort of method which is, or at least comes near to, what may be termed a natural one,[d1] are actually to be found. We there read of '*corporal injuries*'; of '*offences against peace*'; against '*health*'; against '*personal security*';[e1] '*liberty*':—'*property*':[3]—light is let in, though irregularly, at various places.

In an unequal imitation of this Synopsis that has lately been performed upon what is called the *Civil Law*,[4] *all* is technical. All, in short, is darkness. Scarce a syllable by which a man would be led to suspect, that the affair in hand were an affair that happiness or unhappiness was at all concerned in.[f1]

[c1] It is that which comprises his IVth Book, entitled PUBLIC WRONGS.

[d1] *Fragmenta methodi naturalis.*—LINNÆI *Phil. Bot.* Tit. *Systematica*, par. 77.[1]

[e1] This title affords a pertinent instance to exemplify the use that a natural arrangement may be of in repelling an incompetent institution. What I mean is the sort of filthiness that is termed *unnatural*. This our Author has ranked in his class of *Offences against 'personal security'*, and, in a subdivision of it, intitled '*Corporal injuries*'.[2] In so doing, then, he has asserted a fact: he has asserted that the offence in question is an offence against personal security; is a corporal injury; is, in short, productive of unhappiness *in that way*. Now this is what, in the case where the act is committed *by consent*, is manifestly not true. *Volenti non fit injuria*. If then the Law against the offence in question had no other title to a place in the system than what was founded on this *fact*, it is plain it would have none. It would be a bad Law altogether. The mischief the offence is of to the community in this case is in truth of quite another nature, and would come under quite another class. When *against* consent, there indeed it does belong really to this class: but then it would come under another name. It would come under that of *Rape*.

[f1] I think it is Selden, somewhere in his *Table-talk*, that speaks of a whimsical notion he had hit upon when a school-boy, that with regard to *Cæsar* and *Justin*, and those other personages of antiquity that gave him so much trouble, there was not a syllable of truth in any thing they said, nor in fact were there ever really any such persons; but that the

---

[1] Carolus Linnaeus (Carl von Linné) (1707–78), *Philosophia Botanica in qua explicantur Fundamenta Botanica*, Stockholm, 1751, 27. Under the title of *Systemata*, para. 77, Linnaeus observes, 'Methodi naturalis Fragmenta studiose inquirenda sunt, primum et ultimum hoc in Botanicis desideratum est.' In a letter to his cousin Samuel Ray, written early in 1767, Bentham refers to his own 'passion' for botany and to 'that System which has made so much noise and occasioned so great a revolution in the Botanical world': *Correspondence* (in *CW*), i, 105.

[2] Blackstone, *Analysis*, Bk. IV, ch. 15 (ed. cit., 115).

[3] Ibid.

[4] The work in question has not been positively identified: Bentham may have been referring to the third edition (1772) of John Taylor's *The Elements of Civil Law*, first published in 1751, though if so, he was mistaken in calling it an 'imitation' of Blackstone's work.

To return, once more, to our Author's Commentaries. Not even in a *censorial* view would I be understood to deem them altogether without merit. For the institutions commented on, where they are capable of good reasons, good reasons are every now and then given: in which way, so far as it goes, one-half of the Censor's task is well accomplished. Nor is the dark side of the picture left absolutely untouched. Under the head of 'Trial by Jury', are some very just and interesting remarks on the yet-remaining imperfections of that mode of trial:[g1] and under that of 'Assurances by matter of Record', on the lying and extortious jargon of *Recoveries*.[h1] So little, however, are these particular remarks of a piece with the general disposition, that shews itself so strongly throughout the work, indeed so plainly adverse to the general maxims that we have seen, that I can scarce bring myself to attribute them to our Author. Not only disorder is announced by them, but remedies, well-imagined remedies, are pointed out. One would think some Angel had been sowing wheat among our Author's tares[i1].[5]

Manner in which the present Essay has been conducted With regard to this Essay itself, I have not much to say. The whole affair was a contrivance of parents to find employment for their children.[1] Much the same sort of notion is that which these technical arrangements are calculated to give us of Jurisprudence: which in them stands represented rather as a game at *Crambo*[2] for Lawyers to whet their wits at, than as that Science which holds in her hand the happiness of nations.

Let us, however, do no man wrong. Where the success has been worse, the difficulty was greater. That detestable chaos of institutions which the Analyst last-mentioned had to do with is still more embarrassed with a technical nomenclature than our own.

[g3] III Comm. Ch. XXIII. p. 387.[3]

[n1] II Comm. Ch. XXI, p. 360.

[i1] The difference between a generous and determined affection, and an occasional, and as it were forced contribution, to the cause of reformation, may be seen, I think, in these Commentaries, compared with another celebrated work on the subject of our Jurisprudence. Mr Barrington, whose agreeable Miscellany has done so much towards opening men's eyes upon this subject[4] Mr Barrington, like an active General in the service of the

---

[1] There is no mention of this 'whimsical notion' in the *Table-talk* (1689) of John Selden (1584–1654), nor has it been traced to any other source available to Bentham. In Jane Austen's *Northanger Abbey*, begun in 1798 though not published until 1818, Catherine Morland tells Henry Tilney (Ch. XIV) that she 'used to think' of historians as 'labouring only for the torment of little boys and girls'.

[2] A game in which one player gives a line to which the other has to find a rhyme without repeating any word in the original line.

[3] This reference should properly be to I Comm. 381–5.

[4] Daines Barrington, *Observations on the Ancient Statutes* (1766).

[5] Cf. Matthew 13:25.

30

principal and professed purpose of it is, to expose the errors and insufficiencies of our Author. The business of it is therefore rather to *overthrow* than to *set up*; which latter task can seldom be performed to any great advantage where the former is the principal one.

To guard against the danger of misrepresentation, and to make sure of doing our Author no injustice, his own words are given all along: and, as scarce any sentence is left unnoticed, the whole comment wears the form of what is called a perpetual one. With regard to a discourse that is simply institutional, and in which the writer builds upon a plan of his own, a great part of the satisfaction it can be made to afford depends upon the order and connection that are established between the several parts of it. In a comment upon the work of another, no such connection, or at least no such order, can be established commodiously, if at all. The order of the comment is prescribed by the order, perhaps the disorder, of the text.

The chief employment of this Essay, as we have said, has necessarily been *to overthrow*. In the little, therefore, which has been done by it in the way of *setting up*, my view has been not so much to think for the Reader, as to put him upon thinking for himself. This I flatter myself with having done on several interesting topics; and this is all that at present I propose.

Among the few positions of my own which I have found occasion to advance, some I observe which promise to be far from popular. These it is likely may give rise to very warm objections: objections which in themselves I do not wonder at, and which in their motive I cannot but approve. The people are a set of masters whom it is not in a man's power in every instance fully to please, and at the same time faithfully to serve. He that is resolved to persevere without deviation in the line of truth and utility, must have learnt to prefer the still whisper of enduring approbation, to the short-lived bustle of tumultuous applause.

Other passages too there may be, of which some farther explanation may perhaps not unreasonably be demanded. But to give these explanations, and to obviate those objections, is a task which, if

Public, storms the strongholds of chicane, wheresoever they present themselves, and particularly fictions, without reserve. Our Author, like an artful partizan in the service of the profession, sacrifices a few, as if it were to save the rest.

Deplorable, indeed, would have been the student's chance for salutary instruction, did not Mr Barrington's work in so many instances, furnish the antidote to our Author's poisons.

executed at all, must be referred to some other opportunity. Consistency forbad our expatiating so far as to lose sight of our Author: since it was the line of his course that marked the boundaries of ours.

Introduction

1. The subject of this examination, is a passage contained in that part of Sir W. Blackstone's Commentaries on the Laws of England, which the Author has styled the Introduction. This Introduction of his stands divided into four Sections. The *first* contains his discourse '*On the* Study *of the* Law'. The *second*, entitled '*Of the* Nature *of* Laws *in general*', contains his speculations concerning the various objects, real or imaginary, that are in use to be mentioned under the common name of Law. The *third*, entitled '*Of the* Laws of England', contains such general observations, relative to these last mentioned Laws, as seemed proper to be premised before he entered into the details of any parts of them in particular. In the *fourth*, entitled, '*Of the* Countries *subject to the* Laws *of* England', is given a statement of the different territorial extents of different branches of those Laws.

Division of our Author's Introduction

2. 'Tis in the *second* of these sections, that we shall find the passage proposed for examination. It occupies in the edition I happen to have before me,[1] which is the *first* (and all the editions, I believe, are paged alike) the space of *seven* pages; from the 47th, to the 53d, inclusive.

What part of it is here to be examined

3. After treating of '*Law in general*', of the '*Law of Nature*', Law of *Revelation*', and '*Law of Nations*', branches of that imaginary whole, our Author comes at length to what he calls '*Law municipal*': that sort of Law, to which men in their ordinary discourse would give the name of Law without addition; the only sort perhaps of them all (unless it be

His definition of Law Municipal

---

[1] 1823 inserts '(1768)', though to what purpose is not clear. The four volumes of the first edition of Blackstone's work appeared between 1765 and 1769, but the date 1768 seems to have no particular relevance here.

that of *Revelation*) to which the name can, with strict propriety, be applied: in a word, that sort which we see made in each nation, to express the will of that body in it which governs. On this subject of LAW *Municipal* he sets out, as a man ought, with a *definition* of the phrase itself; an important and fundamental phrase, which stood highly in need of a definition, and never so much as since our Author has defined it.

A digression in the middle of it. Its general contents
4. This definition is ushered in with no small display of accuracy. First, it is given entire: it is then taken to pieces, clause by clause; and every clause by itself, justified and explained. In the very midst of these explanations, in the very midst of the definition, he makes a sudden stand. And now it bethinks him that it is a good time to give a dissertation, or rather a bundle of dissertations, upon various subjects—On the *manner* in which *Governments were* established—On the different *forms* they assume when they *are* established—On the peculiar excellence of that form which is established in *this country*—On the *right*, which he thinks it necessary to tell us, the GOVERNMENT in every country has of making LAWS—On the *duty* of making LAWS; which, he says, is also incumbent on the Government.—In stating these two last heads, I give, as near as possible, his own *words*; thinking it premature to engage in discussions, and not daring to decide without discussion on the *sense*.

This disgression the subject of the present examination
5. The digression we are about to examine, is, as it happens, not at all involved with the body of the work from which it starts. No mutual references or allusions: no supports or illustrations communicated or received. It may be considered as one small work inserted into a large one; the contain*ing* and the contain*ed*, having scarce any other connection than what the operations of the press have given them. It is this disconnection that will enable us the better to bestow on the latter a separate examination, without breaking in upon any thread of reasoning, or any principle of Order.

Our Author's sketch of the contents
6. A general statement of the topics touched upon in the digression we are about to examine has been given above. It will be found, I trust, a faithful one. It will not be thought, however, much of a piece, perhaps, with the following, which our Author himself has given us. 'This', (says he,[a] meaning an explanation he had been giving of a part of the definition above spoken of) 'will naturally lead us into a short

[a] I Comm. p. 47.

enquiry into the nature of society and civil government;[b] and the natural inherent right that belongs to the sovereignty of a state, wherever that sovereignty be lodged, of making and enforcing Laws.'

/ 7. No very explicit mention here, we may observe, of the *manner* in which governments have been established, or of the different *forms* they assume when established: no very explicit intimation that these were among the topics to be discussed. None at all of the *duty* of government to make laws; none at all of the *British constitution*; though, of the four other topics we have mentioned, there is no one on which he has been near so copious as on this last. The *right* of Government to make laws, that delicate and invidious topic, as we shall find it when explained, is that which for the moment, seems to have swallowed up almost the whole of his attention.

8. Be this as it may, the contents of the dissertation before us, taken as I have stated them, will furnish us with the matter of five chapters:—one, which I shall entitle 'FORMATION *of* GOVERN-MENT'—a second, 'FORMS *of* GOVERNMENT'—a third, 'BRITISH CONSTITUTION'—a fourth, 'RIGHT *of the* SUPREME POWER *to make* LAWS'—a fifth, 'DUTY *of the* SUPREME POWER *to make* LAWS'.

Inadequate

Division of the present Essay

[b] To make sure of doing our Author no injustice, and to shew what it is that he thought would 'naturally lead us into' this 'enquiry,' it may be proper to give the paragraph containing the explanation above mentioned. It is as follows:—'But farther: municipal law is a rule of civil conduct, prescribed *by the supreme power in a state*.' 'For legislature, as was before observed, is the greatest act of superiority that can be exercised by one being over another. Wherefore it is requisite, to the very essence of a law, that it be made' (he might have added, *or at least supported*) 'by the supreme power. Sovereignty and legislature are indeed convertible terms; one cannot subsist without the other.' I Comm. p. 46.

CHAPTER I
Formation of Government

Subject of the passage to be examined in the present chapter 1. The first object which our Author seems to have proposed to himself in the dissertation we are about to examine, is to give us an idea of the *manner* in which Governments were formed. This occupies the first paragraph, together with part of the second: for the *typographical* division does not seem to quadrate very exactly with the *intellectual*. As the examination of this passage will unavoidably turn in great measure upon the words, it will be proper the reader should have it under his eye.

The passage recited 2. 'The only true and natural foundations of *society*,' (says our Author)[a] 'are the wants and the fears of individuals. Not that we can believe, with some theoretical writers, that there ever was a time when there was no such thing as *society*; and that, from the impulse of reason, and through a sense of their wants and weaknesses, individuals met together in a large plain, entered into an *original contract*, and chose the tallest man present to be their governor. This notion of an actually existing unconnected *state of nature*, is too wild to be seriously admitted; and besides, it is plainly contradictory to the revealed accounts of the primitive origin of mankind, and their preservation two thousand years afterwards; both which were effected by the means of single families. These formed the first *society*, among themselves; which every day extended its limits, and when it grew too large to subsist with convenience in that pastoral state, wherein the Patriarchs appear to have lived, it necessarily subdivided itself by various migrations into more. Afterwards, as agriculture increased,

[a] I Comm. p. 47.

36

which employs and can maintain a much greater number of hands, migrations became less frequent; and various tribes which had formerly separated, re-united again; sometimes by compulsion and conquest, sometimes by accident, and sometimes perhaps by compact. But though *society* had not its formal beginning from any convention of individuals, actuated by their wants and their fears; yet it is the *sense* of their weakness and imperfection that *keeps* mankind together; that demonstrates the necessity of this union; and that therefore is the solid and natural foundation, as well as the cement of *society*: And this is what we mean by the *original contract of society*; which, though perhaps in no instance it has ever been formally expressed at the first institution of a state, yet in nature and reason must always be understood and implied, in the very act of associating together: namely, that the whole should protect all its parts, and that every part should pay obedience to the will of the whole; or, in other words, that the community should guard the rights of each individual member, and that (in return for this protection) each individual should submit to the laws of the community; without which submission of all it was impossible that protection could be certainly extended to any.'

'For when *society* is once formed, *government* results of course, as necessary to preserve and to keep that *society* in order. Unless some superior were constituted, whose commands and decisions all the members are bound to obey, they would still remain as in a *state of nature*, without any judge upon earth to define their several rights, and redress their several wrongs.[1]—Thus far our Author.

3. When leading terms are made to chop and change their several significations; sometimes meaning one thing, sometimes another, at the upshot perhaps nothing; and this in the compass of a paragraph; one may judge what will be the complexion of the whole context. This, we shall see, is the case with the chief of those we have been reading: for instance, with the words 'Society',—'State of nature',—original contract',—not to tire the reader with any more. '*Society*', in one place means the same thing as '*a state of nature*' does: in another place it means the same as '*Government*'. Here, we are required to believe there *never was* such a state as a state of nature: there we are given to understand there *has been*. In like manner with respect to an

Confusion among the leading terms of it

---

[1] I Comm. 47–8, which however reads 'be' for 'were' in the first clause of the final sentence.

original contract we are given to understand that such a thing never existed; that the notion of it is ridiculous: at the same time that there is no speaking nor stirring without supposing there was one.

'Society' put synonymous to a state of nature— opposed to 'Government'— and spoken of as having existed

4. 1*st*, Society means a *state of nature*. For if by '*a state of nature*' a man means any thing, it is the state, I take it, men are in or supposed to be in, before they are under *government*: the state men quit when they enter into a state of government; and in which were it not for government they would remain. But by the word '*society*' it is plain at one time that he means that state. First, according to him, comes *society*; then afterwards comes *government*. 'For when society', says our Author, 'is once formed, government results of course; as necessary to preserve and keep that society in order.'[b]—And again, immediately afterwards,—'A state in which a superior has been constituted, whose commands and decisions all the members are bound to obey', he puts as an explanation (nor is it an inapt one) of a state of '*government*': and 'unless' men were in a state of that description, they would still 'remain', he says, 'as in a *state of nature*'. By *society*, therefore, he means, once more, the same as by a '*state of nature*': he *opposes* it to *government*. And he speaks of it as a state which, in this sense, has actually existed.

'Society' put synonymous to 'government'

5. 2*dly*, This is what he tells us in the beginning of the *second* of the two paragraphs: but all the time the *first* paragraph lasted, *society* meant the same as *government*. In shifting then from one paragraph to another, it has changed its nature. 'Tis 'the foundations of *society*',[c] that he first began to speak of, and immediately he goes on to explain to us, after his manner of explaining, the foundations of *government*. 'Tis of a 'formal beginning' of 'Society',[d] that he speaks soon after; and by this formal beginning, he tells us immediately, that he means, 'the *original contract* of *society*',[e] which contract entered into, 'a *state*',[f] he gives us to understand, is thereby 'instituted', and men have undertaken to 'submit to Laws'.[g] So long then as this first paragraph

[b] v. supra p. 426.[1]
[d] I Comm. p. 47. supra p. 426.
[f] I Comm. p. 47. supra p. 425.

[c] I Comm. p. 47.
[e] I Comm. p. 47. supra p. 425.
[g] I Comm. p. 48. supra p. 426.

---

[1] This footnote is omitted by Montague, followed by Harrison. 1823 retains it but fails to adjust the 1776 page-reference (p. 11) to its own pagination, as had been done in the Dublin edn. Montague and Harrison also omit, in nn. d–1 below, Bentham's page-references to his own quotation from Blackstone's text. Dublin and 1823 both include these, with appropriate adjustments.

lasts, *'society'*, I think, it is plain cannot but have been meaning the same as *'government'*.

6. 3*dly*, All this while too, this same *'state of nature'* to which we have seen *'Society'* (a state spoken of as existing) put synonymous, and in which were it not for *government*, men, he informs us, in the next page, would *'remain'*,[h] is a state in which they never *were*. So he expressly tells us. This 'notion', says he, 'of an actually existing unconnected state of nature'; (that is, as he explains himself afterwards,[i] 'a state in which men have no judge to define their rights, and redress their wrongs), is too wild to be seriously admitted'.[j] When he admits it then himself, as he does in his next page, we are to understand, it seems, that he is bantering us: and that the next paragraph is (what one should not otherwise have taken if for) a piece of pleasantry. *A state of nature spoken of, as never having existed*

7. 4*thly*, The *original contract* is a thing, we are to understand, that never had existence; perhaps not in *any* state: certainly therefore not in *all*. 'Perhaps, in no instance', says our Author, 'has it ever been formally expressed at the first institution of a state.'[k] *Original contract. its reality denied—*

8. 5*thly*, Notwithstanding all this, we must suppose, it seems, that it had in *every* state: 'yet in nature and reason', (says our Author) 'it must always be understood and implied'.[l] Growing bolder in the compass of four or five pages, where he is speaking of our own Government, he asserts roundly,[m] that such a Contract was actually made at the first formation of it. 'The legislature would be changed', he says, 'from that which *was originally* set up by the general consent and fundamental act of the society.' *—asserted*

9. Let us try whether it be not possible for something to be done towards drawing the import of these terms out of the mist in which our Author has involved them. The word 'SOCIETY', I think it appears, is used by him, and that without notice, in two senses that are opposite. In the one, SOCIETY, or a STATE of SOCIETY, is put *synonymous* to a STATE of NATURE; and stands *opposed* to GOVERNMENT, or a STATE OF GOVERNMENT: in this sense, it may be styled, as it commonly is, *natural* SOCIETY. In the other, it is put *synonymous* to GOVERNMENT, or a STATE OF GOVERNMENT; and stands *opposed* to a STATE OF NATURE. In this sense it may be styled, as it commonly is, *Attempt to reconcile these contradictions— Society distinguished into natural and political*

---

[h] I Comm. p. 48. supra p. 426.
[j] I Comm. p. 47. supra p. 425.
[l] I Comm. p. 46. supra p. 426.

[i] I Comm. p. 48. supra p. 425.
[k] I Comm. p. 46. supra p. 426.
[m] I Comm. p. 52.

political SOCIETY. Of the difference between these two states, a tolerably distinct idea, I take it, may be given in a word or two.

Idea of political *society*

10. The idea of a natural society is a *negative* one. The idea of a political society is a *positive* one. 'Tis with the latter, therefore, we should begin.

When a number of persons (whom we may style *subjects*) are supposed to be in the *habit* of paying *obedience* to a person, or an assemblage of persons, of a known and certain description (whom we may call *governor* or *governors*) such persons altogether (*subjects* and *governors*) are said to be in a state of *political* SOCIETY.[n]

Idea of natural *society*

11. The idea of a state of *natural* SOCIETY is, as we have said, a *negative* one. When a number of persons are supposed to be in the habit of *conversing* with each other, at the same time that they are not in any such habit as mentioned above, they are said to be in a state of *natural* SOCIETY.

Difficulty of drawing the line between the two states

12. If we reflect a little, we shall perceive, that, between these two states, there is not that explicit separation which these names, and these definitions might teach one, at first sight, to expect. It is with them as with light and darkness: however distinct the ideas may be, that are, at first mention, suggested by those *names*, the *things* themselves have no determinate bound to separate them. The circumstance that has been spoken of as constituting the difference between these two states, is the presence or absence of an *habit of obedience*. This habit, accordingly, has been spoken of simply as *present* (that is as being *perfectly* present) or, in other words, we have spoken as if there were a *perfect* habit of obedience, in the *one* case: it has been spoken of simply as *absent* (that is, as being *perfectly* absent) or, in other words, we have spoken as if there were *no* habit of obedience at all, in the *other*. But neither of these manners of speaking, perhaps, is strictly just. Few, in fact, if any, are the instances of this habit being perfectly *absent*; certainly none at all, of its being perfectly *present*. Governments accordingly, in proportion as the habit of obedience is more perfect, recede from, in proportion as it is less perfect, approach to, a state of nature: and instances may present themselves in which it shall be difficult to say whether a habit, perfect, in the degree in which, to constitute a government, it is deemed necessary it *should* be perfect, *does* subsist or *not*.[o]

---

[n] V. infra, par. 12, note o.

1. A habit [o] 1. A *habit* is but an assemblage of *acts*: under which name I would also include, for the present, *voluntary forebearances*.

2. A *habit of obedience* then is an assemblage of *acts of obedience*.

3. An *act of obedience* is any act done in pursuance of an *expression of will* on the part of some *superior*.

4. An *act of* POLITICAL *obedience* (which is what is here meant) is any act done in pursuance of an expression of will on the part of a person governing.

5. An *expression of will* is either *parole* or *tacit*.

6. A *parole expression of will* is that which is conveyed by the *signs* called *words*.

7. A *tacit expression of will* is that which is conveyed by any other *signs* whatsoever: among which none are so efficacious as *acts of punishment* annexed in time past, to the non-performance of acts of the same sort with those that are the objects of the will that is in question.

8. A *parole* expression of the will of a superior is a *command*.

9. When a *tacit* expression of the will of a superior is supposed to have been uttered, it may be styled a *fictitious command*.

10. Were we at liberty to coin words after the manner of the Roman lawyers, we might say a *quasi*-command.

11. The STATUTE LAW is composed of *commands*. The COMMON LAW, of *quasi*-commands.

12. An act which is the object of a command actual or fictitious; such an act, considered before it is performed, is styled a *duty*, or a *point of duty*.

13. These definitions premised, we are now in a condition to give such an idea, of what is meant by the *perfection* or *imperfection* of a *habit of obedience* in a society as may prove tolerably precise.

14. A *period* in the duration of the society; the number of *persons* it is composed of during that period; and the number of *points of duty* incumbent on each person being given;—the habit of obedience will be more or less *perfect*, in the ratio of the number of acts of *obedience* to those of *disobedience*.

15. The habit of obedience in this country appears to have been more perfect in the time of the Saxons than in that of the Britons: unquestionably it is more so now than in the time of the Saxons. It is not yet so perfect, as well contrived and well digested laws in time, it is to be hoped, may render it. But absolutely perfect, till man ceases to be man, it never *can* be.

A very ingenious and instructive view of the progress of nations, from the least perfect states of political union to that highly perfect state of it in which we live, may be found in LORD KAIMS's *Historical Law Tracts*.[1]

---

[1] Lord Kames, *Historical Law-Tracts* (1758). Bentham's reference here is apparently to Tract No. I, on the history of the criminal law, in Vol. i, 28 ff.

A perfect state of nature not more chimerical than a perfect state of government

13. On these considerations, the supposition of a *perfect state of nature*, or, as it may be termed, a state of *society perfectly natural*, may, perhaps, be justly pronounced, what our Author for the moment seemed to think it, an extravagant supposition: but then that of a *government* in this sense *perfect*; or, as it may be termed, a state of society *perfectly political*, a state of *perfect political union*, a state of *perfect submission* in the *subject*, of *perfect authority* in the *governor*, is no less so.[P]

16. Political union or connection

16. For the convenience and accuracy of discourse it may be of use, in this place to settle the signification of a few other expressions relative to the same subject. Persons who, with respect to each other, are in a state of *political society*, may be said also to be in a state of *political union* or *connection*.

17. Submission— subjection

17. Such of them as are *subjects* may, accordingly, be said to be in a state of *submission*, or of *subjection*, with respect to *governors*: such as are *governors* in a state of *authority* with respect to *subjects*.

18. Submission x subjection[1]

18. When the subordination is considered as resulting originally from the *will*, or (it may be more proper to say) the *pleasure* of the party govern*ed*, we rather use the word '*submission*:' when from that of the party govern*ing*, the word '*subjection*.' On this account it is, that the term can scarcely be used without apology, unless with a note of disapprobation: especially in this country, where the habit of considering the *consent* of the persons govern*ed* as being in some sense or other involved in the notion of all *lawful*, that is, all *commendable* government, has gained so firm a ground. It is on this account, then, that the term '*subjection*,' *ex*cluding as it does, or, at least, not *in*cluding such consent, is used commonly in what is called a BAD sense: that is, in such a sense as, together with the idea of the object in question, conveys the *accessary* idea of disapprobation. This accessary idea, however, annexed as it is to the *abstract* term 'subjection,' does not extend itself to the *concrete* term 'subjects'—a kind of inconsistency of which there are many instances in language.

It is not a family union, however perfect, that can constitute a political society—why

[P] It is true that every person must, for some time, at least, after his birth, necessarily be in a state of subjection with respect to his parents, or those who stand in the place of parents to him; and that a perfect one, or at least as near to being a perfect one, as any that we see. But for all this, the sort of society that is constituted by a state of subjection thus circumstanced, does not come up to the idea that, I believe, is generally entertained by those who speak of a *political* society. To constitute what is meant in general by that phrase, a greater *number* of members is required, or, at least, a *duration* capable of a longer continuance. Indeed, for this purpose nothing less, I take it, than an *indefinite* duration is required. A society, to come within the notion of what is originally meant by a *political* one, must be such as, in its nature, is not incapable of continuing for ever in virtue of the principles which gave it birth. This, it is plain, is not the case with such a family society, of which a parent, or a pair of parents are at the head. In such a society, the only principle of union which is certain and uniform in its operation, is the natural weakness of those of its members that are in a state of subjection; that is, the children; a

---

[1] Montague, followed by Harrison, replaces the symbol by a dash here, having omitted it altogether at nos. 10 and 11 above.

14. A remark there is, which, for the more thoroughly clearing up of our notions on this subject, it may be proper here to make. To some ears, the phrases, 'state of nature,' 'state of political society,' may carry the appearance of being *absolute* in their signification: as if the condition of a man, or a company of men, in one of these states, or in the other, were a matter that depended altogether upon themselves. But this is not the case. To the expression 'state of nature,' no more than to the expression 'state of political society,' can any precise meaning be annexed, without reference to a party different from that one who is spoken of as being in the state in question. This will readily be perceived. The difference between the two states lies, as we have observed, in the *habit of obedience*. With respect then to a habit of obedience, it can neither be understood as subsisting in any person, nor as not subsisting in any person, but with reference to some other person. For one party to *obey*, there must be another party that is obey*ed*. But this party who is obeyed, may at different times be different. Hence may one and the same party be conceived to obey and *not* to obey at the same time, so as it be with respect to different *persons*, or as we may say, to different *objects of obedience*. Hence it is, then, that one and the same party may be said to *be* in a state of nature, and *not* to be in a state of nature, and that at one and the same time, according as it is this or *that* party that is taken for the other object of comparison. The case is, that in common speech, when no particular object of comparison is specified, all persons in general are intended: so that when a number of persons are said simply to be in a state of nature, what is understood is, that they are so as well with reference to one another, as to all the world.

15. In the same manner we may understand, how the same man, who is *governor* with respect to one man or set of men, may be *subject* with respect to another: how among governors some may be in a

'State of nature' a relative expression

Different degrees of subjection among governors

principle which has but a short and limited continuance. I question whether it be the case even with a family society, subsisting in virtue of *collateral* consanguinity; and that for the like reason. Not but that even in this case a habit of obedience, as perfect as any we see examples of, may subsist for a time; to wit, in virtue of the same *moral* principles which may protract a habit of *filial* obedience beyond the continuance of the *physical* ones which gave birth to it: I mean affection, gratitude, awe, the force of habit, and the like. But it is not long, even in this case, before the bond of connection must either become imperceptible or lose its influence by being too extended.

These considerations, therefore, it will be proper to bear in mind in applying the definition of political society above given (in par. 10) and in order to reconcile it with what is said further on (in par. 17).

perfect state of *nature*, with respect to each other: as the KINGS of FRANCE and SPAIN: others, again, in a state of *perfect subjection*, as the HOSPODARS of WALACHIA and MOLDAVIA with respect to the GRAND SIGNIOR[1]: others, again, in a state of manifest but *imperfect subjection*, as the GERMAN States with respect to the EMPEROR: others, again, in such a state in which it may be difficult to determine whether they are in a state of *imperfect subjection* or in a *perfect* state of *nature*: as the KING of NAPLES with respect to the POPE.[q]

The same person alternately in a state of political and natural society with respect to different societies

16. In the same manner, also, it may be conceived, without entering into details, how any single person, born, as all persons are, into a state of perfect subjection to his parents,[r] that is into a state of perfect political society with respect to his parents, may from thence pass into a perfect state of nature; and from thence successively into any number of different states of political society more or less perfect, by passing into different societies.

In the same political society the same persons alternately governors and subjects, with respect to the same persons

17. In the same manner also it may be conceived how, in any political society, the same man may, with respect to the same individuals, be, at different periods, and on different occasions, alternately, in the state of governor and subject: to-day concurring, perhaps active, in the business of issuing a *general* command for the observance of the whole society, amongst the rest of another man in quality of *Judge*: to-morrow, punished, perhaps, by a *particular* command of that same Judge for not obeying the general command which he himself (I mean the person acting in character of governor) had issued. I need scarce remind the reader how happily this alternate state of *authority* and submission is exemplified among ourselves.

Hints of several topics that must be passed by

18. Here might be a place to state the different shares which different persons may have in the issuing of the same command: to

[q] The Kingdom of Naples is feudatory to the Papal See: and in token of fealty, the King, at his accession, presents the Holy Father with a white horse. The Royal vassal sometimes treats his Lord but cavalierly: but always sends him his white horse.[2]
[r] V. supra, par. 13, note *p*.

---

[1] Early in the 18th century the rule of the Moldavian and Wallachian princes (who had paid tribute to the Ottoman Empire since the 16th century) was replaced by the direct administration of the hospodars – commonly Phanariot Greeks from Constantinople. By the treaty of Küchük Kaynarja (1774) Russia had secured the imposition of certain conditions on the Sultan's government of the Romanian provinces.
[2] The papal claim to suzerainty over the kingdom of Naples and Sicily dated from 1059, when Pope Nicholas II invested the Norman Robert Guiscard with the lands he had acquired in southern Italy.

explain the nature of *corporate action*: to enumerate and distinguish half a dozen or more different modes in which *subordination* between the same parties may subsist: to distinguish and explain the different senses of the words, '*consent*', '*representation*', and others of connected import: *consent* and *representation*, those interesting but perplexing words, sources of so much debate: and sources or pretexts of so much animosity. But the limits of the present design will by no means admit of such protracted and intricate discussions.

19. In the same manner, also, it may be conceived, how the same set of men considered *among themselves*, may at one time be in a state of nature, at another time in a state of government. For the habit of obedience, in whatever degree of perfection it be necessary it should subsist in order to constitute a government, may be conceived, it is plain, to suffer interruptions. At different junctures it may take place and cease. *The same society alternately in a state of nature and a state of government*

20. Instances of this state of things appear not to be unfrequent. The sort of society that has been observed to subsist among the AMERICAN INDIANS may afford us one. According to the accounts we have of those people, in most of their tribes, if not in all, the habit we are speaking of appears to be taken up only in time of war. It ceases again in time of peace. The necessity of acting in concert against a common enemy, subjects a whole tribe to the orders of a common Chief. On the return of peace each warrior resumes his pristine independence. *Instance the Aborigines of America*

21. One difficulty there is that still sticks by us. It has been started indeed, but not solved.—This is to find a note of distinction,—a characteristic mark, whereby to distinguish a society in which there *is* a habit of obedience, and that at the degree of perfection which is necessary to constitute a state of government, from a society in which there is *not*: a mark, I mean, which shall have a visible determinate commencement; insomuch that the instant of its first appearance shall be distinguishable from the last at which it had not as yet appeared. 'Tis only by the help of such a mark that we can be in a condition to determine, at any given time, whether any given society is in a state of government, or in a state of nature. I can find no such mark, I must confess, any where, unless it be this; the establishment of names of office: the appearance of a certain man, or set of men, with a certain name, serving to mark them out as objects of obedience: such as King, Sachem, Cacique, Senator, Burgomaster, and the *Characteristic of political union*

45

like.[1] This, I think, may serve tolerably well to distinguish a set of men in a state of political union among *themselves* from the *same* set of men not yet in such a state.

Among persons already in a state of political union at what instant a new society can be said to be formed, by defection from a former

22. But suppose an incontestable political society, and that a large one, formed; and from that a smaller body to break off: by this breach the smaller body ceases to be in a state of political union with respect to the larger: and has thereby placed itself, with respect to that larger body, in a state of nature—What means shall we find of ascertaining the precise juncture at which this change took place? What shall be taken for the *characteristic mark* in this case? The appointment, it may be said, of new governors with new names. But no such appointment, suppose, takes place. The subordinate governors, from whom alone the people at large were in use to receive their commands under the old government, are the same from whom they receive them under the new one. The habit of obedience which these subordinate governors were in with respect to that single person, we will say, who was the supreme governor of the whole, is broken off insensibly and by degrees. The old names by which these subordinate governors were characterized, while they were subordinate, are continued now they are supreme. In this case it seems rather difficult to answer.

1st, in case of defection by whole bodies, instance the Dutch provinces

23. If an example be required, we may take that of the DUTCH provinces with respect to SPAIN. These provinces were once branches of the Spanish monarchy. They have now, for a long time, been universally spoken of as independent states: independent as well of that of Spain as of every other. They are now in a state of nature with respect to Spain. They were once in a state of political union with respect to Spain: namely, in a state of subjection to a single *governor*, a King, who was King of Spain. At what precise juncture did the dissolution of this political union take place? At what precise time did these provinces cease to be subject to the King of Spain? This, I doubt, will be rather difficult to agree upon.[s]

---

[s] Upon recollection, I have some doubt whether this example would be found historically exact. If not, that of the defection of the Nabobs of Hindostan[2] may answer the purpose. My first choice fell upon the former; supposing it to be rather better known.

---

[1] A sachem was a chief among certain North American Indians, a cacique among the aboriginal inhabitants of the Caribbean islands and in neighbouring parts of the American mainland.

[2] During the decline and disintegration of the Mogul power in India in the early part of the 18th century.

24. Suppose the defection to have begun, not by entire provinces, as in the instance just mentioned, but by a handful of fugitives, this augmented by the accession of other fugitives, and so, by degrees, to a body of men too strong to be reduced, the difficulty will be increased still farther. At what precise juncture was it that ancient ROME, or that modern VENICE, became an independent state?

2dly, in case of defection, by individuals— instances. Rome—Venice

25. In general then, at what precise juncture is it, that persons subject to a government, become, by disobedience, with respect to that government, in a state of nature? When is it, in short, that a *revolt* shall be deemed to have taken place; and when, again, is it, that that revolt shall be deemed to such a degree successful, as to have settled into *independence?*

A revolt, at what juncture it can be said to have taken place

26. As it is the obedience of individuals that constitutes a state of submission, so is it their disobedience that must constitute a state of revolt. Is it then every act of disobedience that will do as much? The afirmative, certainly, is what can never be maintained: for then would there be no such thing as government to be found any where. Here then a distinction or two obviously presents itself. Disobedience may be distinguished into *conscious* or *unconscious*: and that, with respect as well to the *law* as to the *fact*.[t] Disobedience that is unconscious with respect to either, will readily, I suppose, be acknowledged not to be a revolt. Disobedience again that is conscious with respect to *both*, may be distinguished into *secret* and *open*; or, in other words, into *fraudulent* and *forcible*.[u] Disobedience that is only fraudulent, will likewise,

Disobediences[2] what do not— amount to a revolt:

---

[t] 1. Disobedience may be said to be *unconscious with respect to the fact*, when the party is ignorant either of his having done the act itself, which is forbidden by the law, or else of his having done it in those *circumstances*, in which alone it is forbidden.

1. Disobedience unconscious with respect to the fact

2. Disobedience may be said to be *unconscious*, with respect to the *law*; when although he may know of his having done the *act* that is in reality forbidden, and that, under the *circumstances* in which it is forbidden, he knows not of its being forbidden in these *circumstances*.

2. Disobedience unconscious with respect to the Law

3. So long as the business of spreading abroad the knowledge of the law continues to lie in the neglect in which it has lain hitherto, instances of disobedience *unconscious with respect to the law*, can never be otherwise than abundant.

3. Illustration

[u] If examples be thought necessary, Theft may serve for an example of *fraudulent* disobedience; Robbery of *forcible*. In Theft, the *person* of the disobedient party, and the

Disobediences fradulent and forcible—the difference, :"·····ited

---

[1] Here and in the marginal heading to par. 27 below, Dublin, followed by Montague, replaces the unusual, but obviously intended plural form '*disobediences*' by the singular. Harrison restores the correct reading (which Dublin and Montague preserve in the analytical table of contents).

I suppose, be readily acknowledged not to amount to a revolt.

Disobediences what do amount to a revolt
27. The difficulty that will remain will concern such disobedience only as is both *conscious*, (and that as well with respect to *law* as *fact*,) and *forcible*. This disobedience, it should seem, is to be determined neither by *numbers* altogether (that is of the persons supposed to be disobedient) nor by *acts*, nor by *intentions*: all three may be fit to be taken into consideration. But having brought the difficulty to this point, at this point I must be content to leave it. To proceed any farther in the endeavour to solve it, would be to enter into a discussion of particular local jurisprudence. It would be entering upon the definition of Treason, as distinguished from Murder, Robbery, Riot, and other such crimes, as, in comparison with Treason, are spoken of as being of a more private nature. Suppose the definition of Treason settled, and the commission of an act of Treason is, as far as regards the person committing it, the characteristic mark we are in search of.

Unfinished state of the above hints
28. These remarks it were easy to extend to a much greater length. Indeed, it is what would be necessary, in order to give them a proper fulness, and method, and precision. But that could not be done without exceeding the limits of the present design. As they are, they may serve as hints to such as shall be disposed to give the subject a more exact and regular examination.

Our Author's proposition, 'That government results of course', not true
29. From what has been said, however, we may judge what truth there is in our Author's observation, that 'when society' (understand *natural* society) 'is once formed, government' (that is political society) (whatever quantity or degree of Obedience is necessary to constitute political society) 'results *of course*; as necessary to preserve and to keep that society in order.' By the words, '*of course*,' is meant, I suppose, *constantly* and *immediately*: at least constantly. According to this, political society, in any sense of it, ought long ago to have been established all the world over. Whether this be the case, let any one judge from the instances of the Hottentots, of the Patagonians, and of so many other barbarous tribes, of which we hear from travellers and navigators.

Ambiguity of the sentence
30. It may be, after all, we have misunderstood his meaning. We have been supposing him to have been meaning to assert a *matter of fact*, and to have written, or at least begun, this sentence in the

act of disobedience, are both endeavoured to be kept secret. In Robbery, the *act* of disobedience, at least, if not the *person* of him who disobeys, is manifest and avowed.

character of an *historical observer*: whereas, all he meant by it, perhaps, was to speak in the character of a *Censor*, and on a case supposed, to express a *sentiment of approbation*. In short, what he meant, perhaps, to persuade us of, was not that 'government' *does actually* 'result' from natural 'society'; but that it were better that it *should*, to wit, as being necessary to 'preserve and keep' men 'in that state of order', in which it is of advantage to them that they should be. Which of the above-mentioned characters he meant to speak in, is a problem I must leave to be determined. The distinction, perhaps, is what never so much as occurred to him; and indeed the shifting insensibly, and without warning, from one of those characters to the other, is a failing that seems inveterate in our Author; and of which we shall probably have more instances than one to notice.

31. To consider the whole paragraph (with its appendage) together, something, it may be seen our Author struggles to over-throw, and something to establish. But *how* it is he would overthrow, or *what* it is he would establish, are questions I must confess myself unable to resolve. 'The preservation of mankind', he observes, 'was effected by single families.' This is what upon the authority of the Holy Scriptures, he assumes; and from this it is that he would have us conclude the notion of an original contract (the same notion which he afterwards adopts) to be ridiculous. The force of this conclusion, I must own, I do not see. Mankind was preserved by single families— Be it so. What is there in this to hinder 'individuals' of those families, or of families descended from those families, from meeting together 'afterwards, in a large plain', or any where else, 'entering into an *original* contract', or any other contract, 'and choosing the tallest man', or any other man, 'present', or absent, to be their Governor? The 'flat contradiction' our Author finds between this supposed transaction and the 'preservation of mankind by single families', is what I must own myself unable to discover. As to the 'actually existing unconnected state of nature' he speaks of, 'the notion of which', he says, 'is too wild to be seriously admitted', whether this be the case with it, is what, as he has given us no notion of it at all, I cannot judge of.

Darkness of the whole paragraph further shewn

32. Something positive, however, in one place, we seem to have. These 'single families,' by which the preservation of mankind was effected; these single families, he gives us to understand, 'formed the first society.' This is something to proceed upon. A society then of the

Further proofs of the darkness of the whole paragraph

one kind or the other; a natural society, or else a political society, was formed. I would here then put a case, and then propose a question. In this society we will say no *contract* had as yet been entered into; no *habit of obedience* as yet formed. Was this then a *natural* society merely, or was it a *political* one? For my part, according to my notion of the two kinds of society as above explained, I can have no difficulty. It was a merely *natural* one. But, according to our Author's notion, which was it? If it *was* already a *political* one, what notion would he give us of such an one as shall have been a *natural* one; and by what change should such precedent natural one have turned into *this* political one? If this was *not* a political one, then what sort of a society are we to understand any one to be which *is* political? By what mark are we to distinguish it from a natural one? To this, it is plain, our Author has not given any answer. At the same time, that to give an answer to it, was, if any thing, the professed purpose of the long paragraph before us.

A general idea of its character

33. It is time this passage of our Author were dismissed—As among the expressions of it are some of the most striking of those which the vocabulary of the subject furnishes, and these ranged in the most harmonious order, on a distant glance nothing can look fairer: a prettier piece of tinsel-work one shall seldom see exhibited from the shew-glass of political erudition. Step close to it, and the delusion vanishes. It is then seen to consist partly of self-evident observations, and partly of contradictions; partly of what every one knows already, and partly of what no one can understand at all.[1]

Difficulty attending this examination

34. Throughout the whole of it, what distresses me is, not the meeting with any positions, such as, thinking them false, I find a difficulty in proving so: but the not meeting with any positions, true, or false, (unless it be here and there a self-evident one,) that I can find a meaning for. If I can find nothing positive to accede to, no more can I to contradict. Of this latter kind of work, indeed, there is the less to do for any one else, our Author himself having executed it, as we have seen, so amply.

The whole of it is, I must confess, to me a riddle: more acute, by far, than I am, must be the Oedipus that can solve it. Happily it is not necessary, on account of any thing that follows, that it should be solved. Nothing is concluded from it. For aught I can find, it has in itself no use, and none is made of it. There it is, and as well might it be any where else, or no where.

---

[1] 1823 omits 'at all'.

35. Were it then possible, there would be no use in its being solved: but being, as I take it, *really* unsolvable, it were of use it should *be seen* to be so. Peace may by this means be restored to the breast of many a desponding student, who, now prepossessed with the hopes of a rich harvest of instruction, makes a crime to himself of his inability to reap what, in truth, his Author has not sown.

Use that may be made of it

36. As to the Original Contract, by turns embraced and ridiculed by our Author, a few pages, perhaps, may not be ill bestowed in endeavouring to come to a precise notion about its reality and use. The stress laid on it formerly, and still, perhaps, by some, is such as renders it an object not undeserving of attention. I was in hopes, however, till I observed the notice taken of it by our author, that this chimera had been effectually demolished by Mr HUME.[v] I think we

Original Contract, a fiction

---

[v] 1. In the third Volume of his TREATISE *on* HUMAN NATURE.[1]

Our Author, one would think, had never so much as opened that celebrated book: of which the criminality in the eyes of some, and the merits in the eyes of others, have since been almost effaced by the splendour of more recent productions of the same pen. The magnanimity of our Author scorned, perhaps, or his circumspection feared, to derive instruction from an enemy: or, what is still more probable, he knew not that the subject had been so much as touched upon by that penetrating and acute metaphysician, whose works lie so much out of the beaten track of Academic reading. But here, as it happens, there is no matter for such fears. Those men, who are most alarmed at the dangers of a free enquiry; those who are most intimately convinced that the surest way to truth is by hearing nothing but on one side, will, I dare answer almost, find nothing of that which they deem poison in this third volume. I would not wish to send the Reader to any other than this, which, if I recollect aright, stands clear of the objections that have of late been urged, with so much vehemence, against the work in general.* As to the two first, the Author himself, I am inclined to think, is not ill disposed, at present, to join with those who are of opinion, that they might, without any great loss to the science of Human Nature, be dispensed with. The like might be said, perhaps, of a considerable part, even of this. But, after all retrenchments, there will still remain enough to have laid mankind under indelible obligations. That the foundations of all *virtue* are laid in *utility*, is there demonstrated, after a few exceptions made, with the strongest force of evidence: but I see not, any more than Helvetius[2] saw, what need there was for the exceptions.

1. Notion of the Original Contract overthrown by Mr HUME

2. For my own part, I well remember, no sooner had I read that part of the work which touches on this subject, than I felt as if scales had fallen from my eyes, I then, for the first time, learnt to call the cause of the people the cause of Virtue.

2. History of a mind perplexed by fiction

*By Dr BEATTIE, in his *Essay on the Immutability of Truth*.

---

[1] Bk. III, pt. II, § VIII, 'Of the Source of Allegiance'.

[2] Hume, op. cit., Bk. III, pt. III, § I, 'Of the Origin of the Natural Virtues and Vices', admitted that some personal qualities, namely those that are 'agreeable' to others or to their possessors, are denominated virtues even though they have no tendency to public merit. Helvétius in *De l'esprit* (1758), II.xiv and xv, argues that true virtues are those of which the practice serves the felicity of the people.

hear not so much of it now as formerly. The indestructible prerogatives of mankind have no need to be supported upon the sandy foundation of a fiction.

Fictions in general mischievous in the present state of things

37. With respect to this, and other fictions, there was once a time, perhaps, when they had their use. With instruments of this temper, I will not deny but that some political work may have been done, and that useful work, which, under the then circumstances of things,

Perhaps a short sketch of the wanderings of a raw but well-intentioned mind, in its researches after moral truth, may, on this occasion, be not unuseful: for the history of one mind is the history of many. The writings of the honest, but prejudiced, Earl of Clarendon[2] to whose integrity nothing was wanting, and to whose wisdom little, but the fortune of living something later; and the contagion of a monkish atmosphere; these, and other concurrent causes, had listed[3] my infant affections on the side of despotism. The Genius of the place I dwelt in,[4] the authority of the state, the voice of the Church in her solemn offices; all these taught me to call Charles a Martyr, and his opponents rebels. I saw innovation, where indeed innovation, but a glorious innovation, was, in their efforts to withstand him. I saw falsehood, where indeed falsehood was, in their disavowals of innovation. I saw selfishness, and an obedience to the call of passion, in the efforts of the oppressed to rescue themselves from oppression. I saw strong countenance lent in the sacred writings to monarchic government: and none to any other. I saw *passive obedience* deep stamped with the seal of the Christian Virtues of humility and self-denial.

Conversing with Lawyers, I found them full of the virtues of their Original Contract, as a recipe of sovereign efficacy for reconciling the accidental necessity of resistance with the general duty of submission. This drug of theirs they administered to me to calm my scruples. But my unpractised stomach revolted against their opiate. I bid them open to me that page of history in which the solemnization of this important contract was recorded. They shrunk from this challenge; nor could they, when thus pressed, do otherwise than our Author has done, confess the whole to be a fiction. This, methought, looked ill. It seemed to me the acknowledgment of a bad cause, the bringing a fiction to support it. 'To prove fiction, indeed,' said I, 'there is need of fiction; but it is the characteristic of truth to need no proof but truth. Have you then really any such privilege as that of coining facts? You are spending argument to no purpose. Indulge yourselves in the licence of supposing that to be true which is not, and as well may you suppose that proposition itself to be true, which you wish to prove, as that other whereby you hope to prove it.' Thus continued I unsatisfying, and unsatisfied, till I learnt to see that *utility* was the test and measure of all virtue; of loyalty as much as any; and that the obligation to minister to general happiness, was an obligation paramount to and inclusive of every other. Having thus got the instruction I stood in need of, I sat down to make my profit of it. I bid adieu to the original contract: and I left it to those to amuse themselves with this rattle, who could think they needed it.

---

[2] Edward Hyde (1609–74), 1st Earl of Clarendon, one of Charles I's principal supporters and chief ministers to Charles II from the Restoration until 1667, began his *History of the Rebellion* while in exile following the Parliamentary victory in the Civil War. It was first printed in 1702–4.

[3] Montague, followed by Harrison, reads 'lifted'; but all the early edns. have the correct reading 'listed', in the sense of 'enlisted'.

[4] Oxford.

could hardly have been done with any other. But the season of *Fiction* is now over: insomuch, that what formerly might have been tolerated and countenanced under that name, would, if now attempted to be set on foot, be censured and stigmatized under the harsher appellations of *incroachment* or *imposture*. To attempt to introduce any *new* one, would be *now* a crime: for which reason there is much danger, without any use, in vaunting and propagating such as have been introduced already. In point of political discernment, the universal spread of learning has raised mankind in a manner to a level with each other, in comparison of what they have been in any former time: nor is any man now so far elevated above his fellows, as that he should be indulged in the dangerous licence of cheating them for their good.

38. As to the fiction now before us, in the character of an *argumentum ad hominem* coming when it did, and managed as it was, it succeeded to admiration. This *had a momentary use*

That compacts, by whomsoever entered into, *ought* to be kept;—that men are *bound* by compacts, are propositions which men, without knowing or enquiring why, were disposed universally to accede to. The observance of promises they had been accustomed to see pretty constantly enforced. They had been accustomed to see Kings, as well as others, behave themselves as if bound by them. This proposition, then, 'that men are bound by *compacts*;' and this other, 'that, if one party performs not his part, the other is released from his,' being propositions which no man disputed, were propositions which no man had any call to prove. In theory they were assumed for axioms: and in practice they were observed as rules.[w] If, on any occasion, it was thought proper to make a shew of proving them, it was rather for form's sake than for any thing else: and that, rather in the way of memento or instruction to acquiescing auditors, than in the way of proof against opponents. On such an occasion the common place retinue of phrases was at hand; *Justice*, *Right Reason* required it, the *Law* of *Nature* commanded it, and so forth; all which are but so many ways of intimating that a man is firmly persuaded of the truth of this or that moral proposition, though he either thinks he *need not*, or finds he *can't*, tell *why*. Men were too obviously and too generally interested in the observance of these rules to entertain doubts concerning the force

---

[w] A *compact* or *contract* (for the two words on this occasion, at least, are used in the same sense) may, I think, be defined, a pair of promises, by two persons reciprocally given, the one promise in consideration of the other. A compact *or* contract

of any arguments they saw employed in their support—It is an old observation how Interest smooths the road to Faith.

Terms of the supposed contract stated

39. A compact, then, it was said, was made by the King and People: the terms of it were to this effect. The People, on their part, promised to the King a *general obedience*. The King, on his part, promised to *govern* the people in such a *particular* manner always, as should be *subservient* to their happiness. I insist not on the words: I undertake only for the sense; as far as an imaginary engagement, so loosely and so variously worded by those who have imagined it, is capable of any decided signification. Assuming then, as a general rule, that promises, when made, ought to be observed; and, as a point of fact, that a promise to this effect in particular had been made by the party in question, men were more ready to deem themselves qualified to judge when it was such a promise was *broken*, than to decide directly and avowedly on the delicate question, when it was that a King acted so far in *opposition* to the happiness of his people, that it were better no longer to obey him.

Stated thus generally, it could not dispense men from entering into the question of utility, as was intended

40. It is manifest, on a very little consideration, that nothing was gained by this manœuvre after all: no difficulty removed by it. It was still necessary, and that as much as ever, that the question men studied to avoid should be determined, in order to determine the question they thought to substitute in its room. It was still necessary to determine, whether the King in question had, or had not acted so far in *opposition* to the happiness of his people, that it were better no longer to obey him; in order to determine, whether the promise he was supposed to have made, had, or had not been broken. For what was the supposed purport of this promise? It was no other than what has just been mentioned.

Nor, if stated more particularly, could it answer what was designed by it

41. Let it be said, that part at least of this promise was to govern in *subservience to Law*: that hereby a more precise rule was laid down for his conduct, by means of this supposal of a promise, than that other loose and general rule to govern in subservience to the *happiness of his people*: and that, by this means, it is the letter of the *Law* that forms the tenor of the rule.

Now true it is, that the governing in opposition to Law, is *one* way of governing in opposition to the happiness of the people: the natural effect of such a contempt of the Law being, if not actually to destroy, at least to threaten with destruction, all those rights and privileges that are founded on it: rights and privileges on the enjoyment of which that happiness depends. But still it is not this that can be safely taken for the entire purport of the promise here in question: and that for several reasons. *First*, Because the most mischievous, and under certain constitutions the most feasible, method of governing in opposition to the happiness of the people, is, by setting the Law itself in opposition to their happiness. *Secondly*, Because it is a case very conceivable, that a King may, to a great degree, impair the happiness of his people without violating the letter of any single Law. *Thirdly*, Because extraordinary occasions may now and then occur, in which the happiness of the people may be better promoted by acting, for the moment, in *opposition* to the Law, than in *subservience* to it. *Fourthly*, Because it is not any single violation of the Law, as such, that can properly be taken for a breach of his part of the contract, so as to be understood to have released the people from the obligation of performing theirs. For, to quit the fiction, and resume the language of plain truth, it is scarce ever any single violation of the Law that, by being *submitted to*, can produce so much mischief as shall surpass the probable mischief of *resisting* it. If every single instance whatever of such a violation were to be deemed an entire dissolution of the contract, a man who reflects at all would scarce find any-where, I believe, under the sun, that Government which he could allow to subsist for twenty years together. It is plain, therefore, that to pass any sound decision upon the question which the inventors of this fiction substituted instead of the true one, the latter was still necessary to be decided. All they gained by their contrivance was, the convenience of deciding it obliquely, as it were, and by a side wind—that is, in a crude and hasty way, without any direct and steady examination.

42. But, after all, for what *reason* is it, that men *ought* to keep their promises? The moment any intelligible reason is given, it is this: that it is for the *advantage* of society they should keep them; and if they do not, that, as far as *punishment* will go, they should be *made* to keep them. It is for the advantage of the whole number that the promises of each individual should be kept: and, rather than they should not be kept, that such individuals as fail to keep them should be punished. If it be asked, how this appears? the answer is at hand:—Such is the benefit to gain, and mischief to avoid, by keeping them, as much more than compensates the mischief of so much punishment as is requisite to oblige men to it. Whether the dependence of *benefit* and *mischief* (that is, of *pleasure* and *pain*) upon men's conduct in this behalf, be as

Nor is it an original independent principle

here stated, is a question of *fact*, to be decided, in the same manner that all other questions of fact are to be decided, by testimony, observation, and experience.[x]

Nor can it serve to prove anything but what may be better proved without it

43. This then, and no other, being the *reason* why men should be made to keep their promises, viz. that it is for the advantage of society that they should, is a reason that may as well be given at once, why *Kings*, on the one hand, in governing, should in general keep within established Laws, and (to speak universally) abstain from all such measures as tend to the unhappiness of their subjects: and, on the other hand, why *subjects* should obey Kings as long as they so conduct themselves, and no longer; why they should obey in short *so long as the probable mischiefs of obedience are less than the probable mischiefs of resistance*: why, in a word, taking the whole body together, it is their *duty* to obey, just so long as it is their *interest*, and no longer. This being the case, what need of saying of the one, that *he* PROMISED so to *govern*; of the other, that they PROMISED so to *obey*, when the fact is otherwise?

The Coronation-oath does not come up to the notion of it

44. True it is, that, in this country, according to ancient forms, some sort of vague promise of *good government* is made by Kings at the ceremony of their coronation: and let the acclamations, perhaps given, perhaps not given, by chance persons out of the surrounding multitude, be construed into a promise of *obedience* on the part of the *whole* multitude: that whole multitude itself, a small drop collected together by chance out of the ocean of the state: and let the two promises thus made be deemed to have formed a perfect *compact*:— not that either of them is declared to be the *consideration* of the other.[y]

---

[x] The importance which the observance of promises is of to the happiness of society, is placed in a very striking and satisfactory point of view, in a little apologue of MONTESQUIEU, entitled, *The History of the Troglodytes*.* The Troglodytes are a people who pay no regard to promises. By the natural consequences of this disposition, they fall from one scene of misery into another; and are at last exterminated. The same Philosopher, in his *Spirit of Laws*, copying and refining upon the current jargon, feigns a LAW for this and other purposes, after defining a LAW to be a *relation*. How much more instructive on this head is the fable of the Troglodytes than the pseudo-metaphysical sophistry of the *Esprit des Loix!*

[y] V. supra par. 38, note *w*.

* See the Collection of his Works.[1]

---

[1] *The History of the Troglodytes* forms Letter XI of Montesquieu's *Lettres persanes* (1721). The history illustrates the miserable consequences of a general disregard of morality and justice, but there is no specific mention of the disregard of promises.

45. Make the most of this concession, one experiment there is, by which every reflecting man may satisfy himself, I think, beyond a doubt, that it is the consideration of *utility*, and no other, that, secretly but unavoidably, has governed his judgment upon all these matters. The experiment is easy and decisive. It is but to reverse, in supposition, in the first place the import of the *particular* promise thus feigned; in the next place, the effect in point of *utility* of the observance of promises *in general*.—Suppose the King to promise that he would govern his subjects *not* according to Law; *not* in the view to promote their happiness:—would this be binding upon *him?* Suppose the people to promise they would obey him *at all events*, let him govern as he will; let him govern to their destruction. Would this be binding upon *them?* Suppose the constant and universal effect of an observance of promises were to produce *mischief*, would it *then* be men's *duty* to observe them? Would it *then* be *right* to make Laws, and apply punishment to *oblige* men to observe them?

The obligation of a promise will not stand against that of utility: while that of utility will against that of a promise

46. 'No;' (it may perhaps be replied) 'but for this reason; among promises, some there are that, as every one allows, are void: now these you have been supposing, are unquestionably of the number. A promise that is in itself *void*, cannot, it is true, create any obligation. But allow the promise to be *valid*, and it is the promise itself that creates the obligation, and nothing else.' The fallacy of this argument it is easy to perceive. For what is it then that the promise depends on for its *validity?* what is it that being *present* makes it *valid?* what is it that being *wanting* makes it *void?* To acknowledge that any *one* promise may be void, is to acknowledge that if any *other is binding*, it is not merely because it is a promise. That circumstance then, whatever it be, on which the validity of a promise depends, that circumstance, I say, and not the promise itself must, it is plain, be the cause of the obligation which a promise is apt in general to carry with it.

A fallacy obviated

47. But farther. Allow, for argument's[1] sake, what we have disproved: allow that the obligation of a promise is independent of every other: allow that a promise is binding *propriâ vi*—Binding then on whom? On him certainly who makes it. Admit this: For what reason is the same individual promise to be binding on those who *never* made it? The King, *fifty years ago*, promised my *Great-Grandfather* to govern him according to Law: my Great-Grandfather, *fifty years ago*, pro-

The obligation of a promise, were it even independent, would not be extensive enough for the purpose

[1] Thus 1776 and 1823. Dublin, followed by Montague and Harrison, reads 'argument'.

mised the King to obey him according to Law. The King, *just now*, promised my *neighbour* to govern him according to Law: my neighbour, *just now*, promised the King to obey him according to Law—Be it so—What are these promises, all or any of them, to *me*? To make answer to this question, some other principle, it is manifest, must be resorted to, than that of the *intrinsic* obligation of promises upon those who make them.

But the principle of UTILITY *is all-sufficient*   **48.** Now this *other* principle that still recurs upon us, what other can it be than the *principle* of UTILITY?[z] The principle which furnishes us

[z] To this denomination, has of late been added, or substituted, the *greatest happiness* or *greatest felicity* principle: this, for shortness, instead of saying at length *that principle* which states the greatest happiness of all those whose interest is in question, as being the right and proper, and only right and proper and universally desirable, *end* of human action: of human action in every situation; and, in particular, in that of a functionary, or set of functionaries, exercising the powers of Government. The word *utility* does not so clearly point to the ideas of *pleasure* and *pain* as the words *happiness* and *felicity* do: nor does it lead us to the consideration of the *number*, of the interests affected: [to][1] the number, as being the circumstance which contributes, in the largest proportion, to the formation of the standard here in question; the *standard of right and wrong*, by which alone the propriety of human conduct, in every situation, can with propriety be tried.

This want of a sufficiently manifest connection between the ideas of *happiness* and *pleasure* on the one hand, and the idea of *utility* on the other, I have every now and then found operating, and with but too much efficiency, as a bar to the acceptance, that might otherwise have been given, to this principle.

For further elucidation of the principle of *utility*, or say *greatest happiness principle*, it may be some satisfaction to the reader, to see a note, inserted in a second edition, now printing, of a later work of the Author's, intitled '*An Introduction to the Principles of Morals and Legislation*'. In chapter I, subjoined to paragraph xiii is a note in these words:—'The principle of utility' (I have heard it said) 'is a dangerous principle: it is dangerous on certain occasions to consult it.' This is as much as to say—what? that it is not consonant to utility to consult utility; in short, that it is *not* consulting it, to consult it.[2]

In the second edition, to this note is added the following paragraph.

Explanation, written 12th July, 1822, relative to the above note.[3]

Not long after the publication of the *Fragment on Government*, Anno 1776, in which, in the character of an all-comprehensive and all-commanding principle, the principle of *utility* was brought to view, one person by whom observation to the above effect was made was *Alexander Wedderburn*, at that time *Attorney* or *Solicitor General*, afterwards

---

[1] 1823 'so': that reading does not seem to fit the context, and the correction has been supplied from *An Introduction to the Principles of Morals and Legislation* (in *CW*, 11n.), where the same material, down to the end of the next paragraph below, was inserted (under the heading 'Note by the Author, July 1822') in the second edition (1823) to which Bentham refers later in the present note. It there figures as a footnote to Ch. I, par. 1.

[2] Op. cit., in *CW*, 14n.

[3] This heading does not appear in this form in the 1823 edition of *An Introduction to the Principles of Morals and Legislation*. There (in *CW*, 14n.) the heading is simply 'Addition by the author, July 1822'.

with that *reason*, which alone depends not upon any higher reason, but which is itself the sole and all-sufficient reason for every point of practice whatsoever.

successively *Chief Justice of the Common Pleas*, and *Chancellor of England*, under the successive titles of *Lord Loughborough* and *Earl of Rosslyn*. It was made—not indeed in my hearing, but in the hearing of a person by whom it was almost immediately communicated to me. So far from being self-contradictory, it was (I now see and confess) a shrewd and perfectly true one. By that distinguished functionary, the state of the Government was perfectly understood; by the obscure individual, at that time, not so much as supposed to be so; his disquisitions had not been as yet applied, with any thing like a comprehensive view, to the field of Constitutional Law, nor therefore to those features of the English Government, by which the greatest happiness of the ruling *one*, with or without that of a favoured few, are now so plainly seen to be the only ends to which the course of it has at any time been directed. The *principle of utility* was an appellative, at that time employed—employed by me, as it has been by others, to designate that which, in a more perspicuous and instructive manner, may as above be designated by the name of the *greatest happiness principle*. 'This principle' (said Wedderburn) 'is a dangerous one.' Saying so, he said that which, to a certain extent, is strictly true; a principle, which lays down, as the only *right* and justifiable end of Government, the greatest happiness of the greatest number—how can it be denied to be a dangerous one? dangerous to every Government, which has for its *actual* end or object, the greatest happiness of a certain *one*, with or without the addition of some comparatively small number of others, whom it is a matter of pleasure or accommodation to him to admit, each of them, to a share in the concern, on the footing of so many junior partners. '*Dangerous*' it therefore really was to the interest—the sinister interest of all those functionaries, himself included, whose interest it was to maximize delay, vexation, and expence, in judicial and other modes of procedure, for the sake of the profit extractible out of the expence. In a Government which had for its end in view the greatest happiness of the greatest number, *Alexander Wedderburn* might have been *Attorney General* and *then Chancellor*, but he would not have been Attorney General with 15,000 *l.* a year, nor Chancellor, with a Peerage, with a veto upon all justice, with 25,000 *l.* a year, and with 500 sinecures at his disposal, under the name of Ecclesiastical Benefices besides *et cœteras*—*Note of the Author's, 12th July, 1822.*[1]

---

[1] This long footnote was the only addition of any substance made by Bentham in the second edition (1823) of *A Fragment on Government*. Apart from minor variations in the use of italics and capitalisation, in paragraphing, and in punctuation, the material which also appeared in *An Introduction to the Principles of Morals and Legislation* differs only in reading 'has' for 'had' in line 36 above (cf. *An Introduction...*, in *CW*, 14 n. d, line 23): the latter reading is probably correct. Wedderburn (1733–1805) was Solicitor-General from 1771 to 1778.

CHAPTER II
Forms of Government

Subject of the present chapter 1. The contents of the whole digression we are examining, were distributed, we may remember, at the outset of this Essay, into five divisions. The first, relative to the manner in which Government in general was formed, has already been examined in the preceding chapter. The next, relative to the different *species* or *forms* it may assume, comes now to be considered.

Theological flourish of our Author 2. The first object that strikes us in this division of our subject is the theological flourish it sets out with. In God may be said, though in a peculiar sense, to be our Author's strength. In theology he has found a not unfrequent source, of ornament to divert us, of authority to overawe us, from sounding into the shallowness of his doctrines[a].[1]

Governors—celestial endowments found for them 3. That governors, of some sort or other, we must have, is what he has been shewing in the manner we have seen in the last chapter. Now for *endowments* to qualify them for the exercise of their function. These endowments then, as if it were to make them shew the brighter, and to keep them, as much as possible, from being soiled by the rough hands of impertinent speculators, he has chosen should be of æthereal texture, and has fetched them from the clouds.

'All mankind',[b] he says, 'will agree that government should be

---

[a] This is what there would be occasion to shew at large, were what he says of LAW in *general*, and of the LAWS of *nature*, and *revelation* in particular, to be examined.
[b] I Comm. p. 48.[2]

---

[1] Thus 1776 and 1823; Dublin, followed by Montague and Harrison, 'doctrine'.
[2] Blackstone's text in fact reads 'grand' for 'great', and the correct reading is reproduced when the passage is repeated below in para. 4.

reposed in such persons in whom those qualities are most likely to be found, the perfection of which are among the attributes of Him who is emphatically styled the Supreme Being: the three great requisites, I mean, of wisdom, of goodness, and of power.'

But let us see the whole passage as it stands—

4. 'But as all the members of Society', (meaning *natural* Society) 'are naturally EQUAL,' (i.e. I suppose, with respect to *political* power, of which none of them as yet have any) 'it may be asked,' (continues he) 'in whose hands are the reins of government to be intrusted? To this the general answer is easy; but the application of it to particular cases, has occasioned one half of those mischiefs which are apt to proceed from misguided political zeal. In general, all mankind will agree that government should be reposed in such persons in whom those qualities are most likely to be found, the perfection of which are among the attributes of Him who is emphatically styled the Supreme Being; the three grand requisites, I mean, of wisdom, goodness, and of power: wisdom, to discern the real interest of the community; goodness, to endeavour always to pursue that real interest; and strength or power, to carry this knowledge and intention into action. These are the natural foundations of sovereignty, and these are the requisites that ought to be found in every well-constituted frame of government.' *The passage recited*

5. Every thing in its place. Theology in a sermon, or a catechism. But in this place, the flourish we have seen, might, for every purpose of instruction, have much better, it should seem, been spared. What purpose the idea of that tremendous and incomprehensible Being thus unnecessarily introduced can answer, I cannot see, unless it were to bewilder and entrance the reader; as it seems to have bewildered and entranced the writer. Beginning thus, is beginning at the wrong end: it is explaining *ignotum per ignotius.* It is not from the attributes of the Deity, that an idea is to be had of any qualities in men: on the contrary, it is from what we see of the qualities of men, that we obtain the feeble idea we can frame to ourselves, of the attributes of the Deity. *Theology on such an occasion as this impertinent*

6. We shall soon see whether it be light or darkness our Author has brought back from this excursion to the clouds. The qualifications he has pitched upon for those in whose hands Government is to be reposed we see are *three*: wisdom, goodness, and power. Now of these three, one there is which, I doubt, will give him some trouble to know *Difficulty it leads him into*

what to do with. I mean that of *Power*: which, looking upon it as a jewel, it should seem, that would give a lustre to the royal diadem, he was for importing from the celestial regions. In heaven, indeed, we shall not dispute its being to be found; and that at all junctures alike. But the parallel, I doubt, already fails. In the earthly governors in question, or, to speak more properly, candidates for government, by the very supposition there can not, at the juncture he supposes, be any such thing. *Power* is that very quality which, in consideration of these other qualities, which, it is supposed, are possessed by them already, they are now waiting to receive.

Power, either natural or political

7. By Power in this place, I, for my part, mean *political* power: the only sort of power our Author could mean: the only sort of power that is here in question. A little farther on we shall find him speaking of this endowment as being possessed, and that in the highest degree, by a King, a single person. *Natural* power therefore, mere organical power, the faculty of giving the hardest blows, can never, it is plain, be that which he meant to number among the attributes of this godlike personage.

In neither sense can it be attributed as he attributes it

8. We see then the dilemma our Author's theology has brought him into, by putting him upon reckoning *power* among the qualifications of his candidates. Power is either *natural* or *political*. *Political* power is what they cannot have by the supposition: for that is the very thing that is to be created, and which by the establishment of Government, men are going to confer on them. If any, then, it must be *natural* power; the natural strength that a man possesses of himself without the help of Government. But of this, then, if this be it, there is more, if we may believe our Author, in a single member of a society, than in that member and all the rest of the society put together.[c]

What it is that may

9. This difficulty, if possible, one should be glad to see cleared up. The truth is, I take it, that in what our Author has said of power, he has been speaking, as it were, by anticipation: and that what he means by it, is not any power of either kind actually possessed by any man, or body of men, at the juncture he supposes, but only a *capacity*, if one may call it so, of *retaining* and *putting* into action political power,

---

[c] V. infra, par. 32 Monarchy, which is the government of *one*, 'is the most powerful form of government,' he says, 'of any:'[1] more so than Democracy, which he describes as being the Government of *all*.

---

[1] I Comm. 50, quoted below.

whensoever it shall have been conferred. Now, of actual power, the quantity that is possessed is, in every case, one and the same: for it is neither more nor less than the supreme power. But as to the capacity above spoken of, there do seem, indeed, to be good grounds for supposing it to subsist in a higher degree in a *single* man than in a *body*.

10. These grounds it will not be expected that I should display at large: a slight sketch will be sufficient.—The efficacy of power is, in part at least, in proportion to the promptitude of obedience: the promptitude of obedience is, in part, in proportion to the promptitude of command:—command is an expression of will: a will is sooner formed by one than many. And this, or something like it, I take to be the plain English of our Author's metaphor, where he tells us,[d] as we shall see a little farther on,[e] that 'a monarchy is the most powerful' (form of government) 'of any, all the sinews of government being knit together, and united in the hands of the prince.' *—and for what reason*

11. The next paragraph, short as it is, contains variety of matter. The first two sentences of it are to let us know, that with regard to the manner in which each of the *particular* governments that we know of have been formed, he thinks proper to pass it by. A third is to intimate, for the second time, that all governments must be absolute in some hands or other. In the fourth and last, he favours us with a very comfortable piece of intelligence; the truth of which, but for his averment, few of us perhaps would have suspected. This is, that the qualifications mentioned by the last paragraph as *requisite* to be possessed by all Governors of states are, or at least once upon a time were, *actually* possessed by them: (i.e.) according to the opinion of somebody; but of what somebody is not altogether clear: whether in the opinion of these Governors themselves, or of the persons governed by them. *Heterogeneous contents of the next paragraph*

12. 'How the several forms of government we now see in the world at first actually began,' says our Author, 'is matter of great uncertainty, and has occasioned infinite disputes. It is not my business or intention to enter into any of them. However they began, or by what right soever they subsist, there is and must be in all of them a supreme, irresistible, absolute, uncontrolled authority, in which the *jura summi imperii*, or the rights of sovereignty, reside. And this authority is placed in those hands, wherein (according to the OPINION *The paragraph recited*

[d] I Comm. p. 50.   [e] Par. 32.

of the FOUNDERS of such respective states, either expressly given or collected from their *tacit* APPROBATION) the qualities requisite for supremacy, wisdom, goodness, and power, are the most likely to be found.'[1]

Paradoxical assertion in the latter part of it, as if all governments were the result of a free preference

13. Who those persons are whom our Author means here by the word *founders*; whether those who became the Govern*ors* of the states in question, or those who became the govern*ed*, or both together, is what I would not take upon me to determine. For aught I know he may have meant neither the one nor the other, but some third person. And, indeed, what I am vehemently inclined to suspect is, that, in our Author's large conception, the mighty and extensive domains of ATHENS and SPARTA, of which we read so much at school and at college, consisting each of several score of miles square, represented, at the time this paragraph was writing, the whole universe: and the respective æras of *Solon* and *Lycurgus*, the whole period of the history of those states.

Reasons for supposing this to have been the meaning of it

14. The words 'founders',—'opinion',—'approbation',—in short the whole complection of the sentence is such as brings to one's view a system of government utterly different from the generality of those we have before our eyes; a system in which one would think neither caprice, nor violence, nor accident, nor prejudice, nor passion, had any share: a system uniform, comprehensive, and simultaneous; planned with phlegmatic deliberation; established by full and general assent: such, in short, as, according to common imagination, were the systems laid down by the two sages above-mentioned. If this be the case, the object he had in mind when he said *Founders*, might be neither Govern*ors* nor govern*ed*, but some *neutral* person: such as those sages, chosen as they were in a manner as umpires, might be considered with regard to the persons who, under the prior constitution, whatever it was, had stood respectively in those two relations.

The doctrine of it applied to particular instances

15. All this, however, is but conjecture: In the proposition itself neither this, nor any other restriction is expressed. It is delivered explicitly and emphatically in the character of an universal one. 'In ALL OF THEM', he assures us, 'this authority,' (the supreme authority) '*is* placed in those hands, wherein, according to the *opinion* of the *founders* of such respective states, these "qualities of wisdom, goodness, and power," are the most likely to be found.' In this character it

[1] I Comm. 48–9.

cannot but throw a singular light on history. I can see no end, indeed, to the discoveries it leads to, all of them equally new and edifying. When the Spaniards, for example, became masters of the empire of Mexico, a vulgar politician might suppose it was because such of the Mexicans as remained unexterminated, could not help it. No such thing[1]—it was because the Spaniards were of 'opinion' or the Mexicans themselves were of 'opinion' (which of the two is not altogether clear) that in Charles Vth, and his successors, more goodness (of which they had such abundant proofs) as well as wisdom, was likely to be found, than in all the Mexicans put together. The same persuasion obtained between Charlemagne and the German Saxons with respect to the goodness and wisdom of Charlemagne:—between William the Norman and the English Saxons:—between Mahomet IId and the subjects of John Paleologus:—between Odoacer and those of Augustulus:—between the Tartar Gingiskan and the Chinese of his time:—between the Tartars Chang-ti and Cam-ghi, and the Chinese of their times:—between the Protector Cromwell and the Scotch:—between William IIId and the Irish Papists:—between Cæsar and the Gauls:—in short, between the Thirty Tyrants, so called, and the Athenians, whom our Author seems to have had in view:—to mention these examples only, out of as many hundred as might be required.[2] All this, if we may trust our Author, he has the '*goodness*' to believe: and by such lessons is the

---

[1] At this point 1776 repeats the latter part ('—applied to particular instances') of the marginal heading above, apparently because the paragraph carried over in the sentence beginning 'No such thing...' to a fresh page. (This was not, however, the printer's usual practice.) In 1823 the arrangement was repeated, with adjustment to the pagination of that edition. Dublin, followed by Montague and Harrison, repeats the insertion without any such adjustment. It is omitted here as having no function.

[2] Bentham's references are to the following: the Spanish conquest of Mexico by Cortes between 1519 and 1521, in the reign of the Emperor Charles V; Charlemagne's subjugation of the Saxons between 772 and 785; the Norman Conquest of England in and after 1066; the final stages of the conflict between the Byzantine Empire (of which John VIII Palaeologus was the last ruler but one, dying in 1448) and the Ottoman Turks under Murad II (1421–51) and Mehmed (Mahomet) II (1451–81), who took Constantinople in 1453; the conquest of Italy by Odovacar (Odoacer) (d. 493) following the dethronement in 476 of Romulus Augustulus as western Emperor; Genghis Khan's invasion of China beginning in 1211; the establishment of the Manchu dynasty in China under the Emperors Shun-chi (1644–61: Chang-ti is his posthumous title) and K'ang-hsi (of which Cam-ghi is a transcription) (1661–72), the word 'Tartar' being frequently used of the Manchus in the 18th century; the subjugation of Scotland by Cromwell in the 1650s and of Ireland by William III in the 1690s; Julius Caesar's campaigns in Gaul 58–50 B.C.; and the regime of the Thirty Tyrants in Athens at the end of the Peloponnesian War in 403 B.C.

General contents of the six remaining paragraphs relating to the subject of this chapter penetration of students to be sharpened for piercing into the depths of politics.

16. So much for the introductory paragraph.—The main part of the subject is treated of in six others: the general contents of which are as follow.

—of the first paragraph— **17.** In the first he tells us how many different forms of government there are according to the division of the antients:[1] which division he adopts. These are three: Monarchy, Aristocracy, and Democracy.

—Second— **18.** The next is to tell us, that by the *sovereign* POWER he means that of '*making laws*'.

—Third— **19.** In a third he gives us the advantages and disadvantages of these three different forms of government.

—Fourth— **20.** In a fourth he tells us that these are all the antients would allow of.

—Fifth— **21.** A Fifth is to tell us that the British form of government is different from each of them; being a combination of all, and possessing the advantages of all.

—Sixth— **22.** In the sixth, and last, he shews us that it could not possess these advantages, if, instead of being what it is, it were either of those others: and tells us what it is that may destroy it. These two last it will be sufficient here to mention: to examine them will be the task of our next chapter.

Definitions of the three sorts of governments according to our Author **23.** Monarchy is that form of Government in which the power of making Laws is lodged in the hands of a *single* member of the state in question. Aristocracy is that form of Government in which the power of making laws is lodged in the hands of *several* members. Democracy is that form of government in which the power of making laws is lodged in the hands of '*all*' of them put together. These, according to our Author, are the definitions of the Antients; and these, therefore, without difficulty, are the definitions of our Author.

The paragraph recited— **24.** 'The political writers of antiquity,' says he, 'will not allow more than three regular forms of government; the first, when the sovereign power is lodged in an aggregate assembly, consisting of all the members of a community, which is called a Democracy; the second, when it is lodged in a council composed of select members, and then it is styled an Aristocracy; the last, when it is entrusted in the hands of

---

[1] Thus 1776 and Dublin, here and in paras. 20 and 23; 1823 and modern edns. read 'ancients', but 1823 preserves 'antients' in paras 20 and 23.

a single person, and then it takes the name of a Monarchy. All other species of government they say are either corruptions of, or reducible to these three.'

25. 'By the sovereign power, as was before observed, is meant the *and the next* making of laws; for wherever that power resides, all others must conform to, and be directed by it, whatever appearance the outward form and administration of the government may put on. For it is at any time in the option of the legislature to alter that form and administration by a new edict or rule, and to put the execution of the laws into whatever hands it pleases; and all the other powers of the state must obey the legislative power in the execution of their several functions, or else the constitution is at an end.'[1]

26. Having thus got three regular simple forms of Government *How he assigns* (this anomalous complex one of our own out of the question) and just *them their* as many qualifications to divide among them; of each of which, by *respective* what he told us a while ago, each form of Government must have *qualifications* some share, it is easy to see how their allotments will be made out. Each form of Government will possess one of these qualities in perfection, taking its chance, if one may say so, for its share in the two others.

27. Among these three different forms of Government then, it *All appearing* should seem according to our Author's account of them, there is not *equally eligible in* much to choose. Each of them has a *qualification*, an *endowment*, to *his view of them* itself. Each of them is completely characterized by this qualification. No intimation is given of any pre-eminence among these qualifications, one above another. Should there be any dispute concerning the preference to be given to any of these forms of government, as proper a method as any of settling it, to judge from this view of them, is that of cross and pile.[2] Hence we may infer, that all the governments that ever were, or will be (except a very particular one that we shall come to presently, that is to say our own) are upon a par: that of ATHENS with that of PERSIA; that of GENEVA with that of MOROCCO: since they are all of them, he tells us, 'corruptions of, or reducible to', one of these. This is happy. A legislator cannot do amiss. He may save himself the expence[3] of thinking. The choice of a king was once determined, we

---

[1] I Comm. 49.
[2] I.e. of pure chance.
[3] Thus 1776, Dublin, 1823; Montague, followed by Harrison, 'expense'.

are told, by the neighing of a horse.[1] The choice of a form of Government might be determined so as well.

Now to the British Constitution

28. As to our own form of government, however, this, it is plain, being that which it seemed good to take for the theme of his panegyric, and being made out of the other three, will possess the advantages of all of them put together; and that without any of the disadvantages; the disadvantages vanishing at the word of command, or even without it, as not being suitable to the purpose.

Contradiction he falls into, in supposing other sorts of government than these three, described as they are by him

29. At the end of the paragraph which gives us the above definitions, one observation there is that is a little puzzling. 'Other species of government', we are given to understand, there are besides these; but then those others, if not 'reducible to', are but 'corruptions of these'. Now, what there is in any of these to be corrupted, is not so easy to understand. The essence of these several forms of government, we must always remember, is placed by him, solely and entirely, in the article of *number*: in the ratio of the number of the Govern*ors*, (for so for shortness we will style those in whose hands is lodged this 'power of making laws') to that of the govern*ed*. If the number of the former be, to that of the latter, as *one* to *all*, then is the form of Government a Monarchy: if as *all* to *all*, then is it a Democracy: if as some number *between one and all* to *all*, then is it an Aristocracy. Now then, if we can conceive a fourth number, which not being more than all, is neither one nor all, nor any thing between one and all, we can conceive a form of Government, which, upon due proof, may appear to be a corruption of some one or other of these three.[f] If not, we must look for the corruption somewhere else: Suppose it were in our Author's *reason*.[g]

---

[f] By the laws of GERMANY, such and such states are to furnish so many men to the general army of the empire: some of them so many men and one half; others, so many and one third; others again, If I mistake not, so many and one fourth.[2] One of these half, third-part, or quarter-men, suppose, possesses himself of the Government: here then we have a kind of corruption of a Monarchy. Is this what our Author had in view?

[g] A more suitable place to look for *corruption* in, if we may take his own word for it, there cannot be. 'Every man's reason,' he assures us* 'is corrupt'; and not only that, but 'his understanding full of ignorance and error'. With regard to others, it were as well not to

*I Comm. p. 41.

---

[1] This is related by Herodotus (iii, 85) of Darius the Great, who was king of Persia from 521 to 485 B.C. and who is said to have agreed with six other princes that he whose horse neighed first should be king.

[2] The army of the Empire had been extensively reorganized in 1681.

30. Not but that we may meet, indeed, with several other hard-worded names for forms of Government: but these names were only so many names for one or other of those three. We hear often of a *Tyranny*: but this is neither more nor less than the name a man gives to our Author's Monarchy, when out of humour with it. It is still the government of number *one*. We hear now and then, too, of a sort of Government called an *Oligarchy*: but this is neither more nor less than the name a man gives to our Author's Aristocracy, in the same case. It is still the Government of some number or other, *between one and all*. In fine, we hear now and then of a sort of government fit to break one's teeth, called an *Ochlocracy*: but this is neither more nor less than the name a man gives to a Democracy in the same case. It is still that sort of government, which, according to our Author, is the Government of *all*.

Governments the same as these under other names

31. Let us now see how he has disposed of his three qualifications among his three sorts or forms of Government. Upon Monarchy, we shall find, he has bestowed the perfection of power; on Aristocracy, of wisdom; on Democracy, of goodness; each of those forms having just enough, we may suppose, of the two remaining qualifications besides its own peculiar one to make up the necessary complement of 'qualities requisite for supremacy.' Kings are, (nay *were* before they were Kings, since it was this qualification determined their subjects to make them Kings[h]), as strong as so many Hercules's; but then, as to their wisdom, or their goodness, there is not much to say. The members of an Aristocracy are so many Solomons: but then they are not such sturdy folks as your Kings; nor, if the truth is to be spoken, have they much more honesty than their neighbours. As to the members of a Democracy, they are the best sort of people in the world; but then they are but a puny sort of gentry, as to strength, put them all together; and are apt to be a little defective in point of understanding.

Qualifications of the three forms, how allotted—the subject resumed

32. 'In a democracy', says he, 'where the right of making laws resides in the people at large, public virtue or goodness of intention, is more likely to be found, than either of the other qualities of government. Popular assemblies are frequently foolish in their contrivance, and weak in their execution; but generally mean to do the

The paragraph recited

---

be too positive: but with regard to a man's self, what he tells us from experience, it would be ill manners to dispute with him.

[h] I Comm. p. 48.

thing that is right and just, and have always a degree of patriotism or public spirit. In aristocracies there is more wisdom to be found than in the other frames of Government; being composed, or intended to be composed, of the most experienced citizens; but there is less honesty than in a republic, and less strength than in a monarchy. A monarchy is indeed the most powerful of any, all the sinews of government being knit together and united in the hand of the prince; but then there is imminent danger of his employing that strength to improvident or oppressive purposes.'[1]

—and the next   **33.** 'Thus these three species of government have all of them their several perfections and imperfections. Democracies are usually the best calculated to direct the end of a law; aristocracies to invent the means by which that end shall be obtained; and monarchies to carry those means into execution. And the antients, as was observed, had in general no idea of any other permanent form of government but these three; for though Cicero declares himself of opinion, *esse optimé constitutam rempublicam, quae ex tribus generibus illis, regali, optimo, et populari sit modicé confusa*; yet Tacitus treats this notion of a mixed government, formed out of them all, and partaking of the advantages of each, as a visionary whim; and one, that if effected, could never be lasting or secure.'[2]

Democracy, as   **34.** In the midst of this fine-spun ratiocination, an accident has
described by him, happened, of which our Author seems not to be aware. One of his
no Government accidents, as a logician would say, has lost its *subject*: one of the
at all   *qualifications* he has been telling us of, is, somehow or other, become vacant: the form of Government he designed it for, having unluckily slipped through his fingers in the handling. I mean Democracy; which he, and, according to him, the Antients, make out to be the Government of *all*. Now '*all*' is a great many; so many that, I much doubt, it will be rather a difficult matter to find these high and mighty personages power enough, so much as to make a decent figure with. The members of this redoubtable Commonwealth will be still worse off, I doubt, in point of subjects, than *Trinculo* in the play,[3] or than the potentates, whom some later navigators found lording it, with might and main, 'ϰρατερῆφι βίηφι',[4] over a Spanish settlement: there were

---

[1] I Comm. 49–50.
[2] I Comm. 50, where the references to Cicero and Tacitus are supplied in footnotes: '*optimo*' should properly read '*optimati*'.
[3] Shakespeare, *The Tempest*, II.ii.
[4] This is a Homeric phrase occurring frequently in the Iliad and the Odyssey. The

three members of the Government; and they had one subject among them all.[i] Let him examine it a little, and it will turn out, I take it, to be precisely that sort of Government, and no other, which one can conceive to obtain, where there is no Government at all. Our Author, we may remember, had shrewd doubts about the existence of a *state of nature*:[j] grant him his Democracy, and it exists in his Democracy.[k]

35. The qualification of *goodness*, I think it was, that belonged to the Government of *all*, while there was such a Government. This having taken its flight, as we have seen, to the region of nonentities, the qualification that was designed for it remains upon his hands: he is at liberty, therefore, to make a compliment of it to Aristocracy or to Monarchy, which best suits him. Perhaps it were as well to give it to Monarchy; the title of that form of Government to its own peculiar qualification, *power*, being, as we have seen, rather an equivocal one: or else, which, perhaps, is as good a way of settling matters as any, he may set them to cast lots.

The qualification designed for it become vacant

[i] See HAWKESWORTH'S *Voyages*.[1]

The condition of these imaginary sovereigns puts one in mind of the story of, I forget what King's Fool. The Fool had stuck himself up one day, with great gravity, in the King's throne with a stick, by way of a sceptre, in one hand, and a ball in the other: being asked what he was doing, he answered, '*reigning*'.[2] Much the same sort of reign, I take it, would be that of the members of our Author's Democracy.

[j] V. supra, ch. I. par. VI.

[k] What is curious is, that the same persons who tell you (having read as much) that Democracy is a form of Government under which the supreme power is vested in all the members of a state, will also tell you (having also read as much) that the Athenian Commonwealth was a Democracy. Now the truth is, that in the Athenian Commonwealth, upon the most moderate computation, it is not one tenth part of the inhabitants of the Athenian state that ever at a time partook of the supreme power: women, children, and slaves, being taken into the account.* Civil Lawyers, indeed, will tell you, with a grave face, that a slave is *nobody*; as Common Lawyers will, that a bastard is the *son* of *nobody*. But, to an unprejudiced eye, the condition of a state is the condition of all the individuals, without distinction, that compose it.

* See, among Mr HUME'S *Essays*, that *on the populousness of ancient nations*.[3]

---

literal meaning – 'with powerful force' – is virtually equivalent to 'with might and main'.

[1] John Hawkesworth (1715–73), *Account of the Voyages undertaken by order of His Present Majesty for Making Discoveries in the Southern Hemisphere*, 3 vols., 1773. No description of a Spanish settlement such as Bentham refers to here has been found in Hawkesworth, though there is a reference in the account of the voyage of the *Dolphin* to a Spanish colony in the Straits of Magellan founded in 1580, where the population was found by an English navigator in 1587 reduced to one man.

[2] This anecdote has not been traced.

[3] David Hume, *Essays Moral Political and Literary*, 1741–2, Pt. II, Essay 17.

CHAPTER III

British Constitution

Our Author's panegyric on the British Constitution **1.** With a set of *data*, such as we have seen in the last chapter, we may judge whether our author can meet with any difficulty in proving the British Constitution to be the best of all possible governments, or indeed any thing else that he has a mind. In his paragraph on this subject there are several things that lay claim to our attention. But it is necessary we should have it under our eye.

The paragraph recited **2.** 'But happily for us in[1] this island the British Constitution has long remained, and I trust will long continue, a standing exception to the truth of this observation. For, as with us the executive power of the laws is lodged in a single person, they have all the advantages of strength and dispatch that are to be found in the most absolute monarchy: and, as the legislature of the kingdom is entrusted to three distinct powers entirely independent of each other; first, the King; secondly, the Lords Spiritual and Temporal, which is an aristocratical assembly of persons selected for their piety, their birth, their wisdom, their valour, or their property; and thirdly, the House of Commons, freely chosen by the people from among themselves, which makes it a kind of democracy; as this aggregate body, actuated by different springs, and attentive to different interests, composes the British Parliament, and has the supreme disposal of every thing; there can no inconvenience be attempted by either of the three branches, but will be withstood by one of the other two; each branch being armed with a negative power sufficient to repel any innovation which it shall think inexpedient or dangerous.'

---

[1] I Comm. 50 reads 'of'.

72

3. 'Here then is lodged the sovereignty of the British Constitution; *—And that* and lodged as beneficially as is possible for society. For in no other *which follows it* shape could we be so certain of finding the three great qualities of Government so well and so happily united. If the supreme power were lodged in any one of the three branches separately, we must be exposed to the inconveniencies of either absolute monarchy, aristocracy, or democracy; and so want two of the principal ingredients of good polity, either virtue, wisdom, or power. If it were lodged in any two of the branches; for instance, in the King and House of Lords, our laws might be providently made and well executed, but they might not always have the good of the people in view: if lodged in the King and Commons, we should want that circumspection and mediatory caution, which the wisdom of the Peers is to afford: if the supreme rights of legislature were lodged in the two Houses only, and the King had no negative upon their proceedings, they might be tempted to encroach upon the royal prerogative, or perhaps to abolish the kingly office, and thereby weaken (if not totally destroy) the strength of the executive power. But the constitutional government of this island is so admirably tempered and compounded, that nothing can endanger or hurt it, but destroy-ing the equilibrium of power between one branch of the legislature and the rest. For if ever it should happen that the independence of any one of the three should be lost, or that it should become subservient to the views of either of the other two, there would[1] soon be an end of our constitution. The legislature would be changed from that which was originally set up by the general consent and fundamental act of the society; and such a change, however effected, is, according to Mr Locke (who perhaps carries his theory too far) at once an entire dissolution of the bands of Government, and the people would be reduced to a state of anarchy, with liberty to constitute to themselves a new legislative power.'[2]

4. In considering the first of these two paragraphs, in the first place, *Executive* the phenomenon we should little expect to see from any thing that *power—the* goes before, is a certain *executive power*, that now, for the first time, *mention of it* bolts out upon us without warning or introduction. *introduced*

The power, the only power our Author has been speaking of all

---

[1] I Comm. 51 reads 'should'.
[2] I Comm. 52 gives the reference to § 212 of Locke's *Second Treatise of Government*.

along till now, is the *legislative*. 'Tis to this, and this alone, that he has given the name of '*sovereign power*'. 'Tis this power, the different distributions of which he makes the characteristics of his three different forms of government. 'Tis with these different distributions, distributions made of the legislative power, that, according to his account, are connected the several qualifications laid down by him, as 'requisites for supremacy': qualifications in the possession of which consist all the advantages which can belong to any form of Government. Coming now then to the British Constitution, it is in the superior degree in which these qualifications of the legislative body are possessed by it, that its peculiar excellence is to consist. It is possessing the qualification of strength, that it possesses the advantage of a monarchy. But how is it then that, by his account, it possesses the qualification of strength? By any disposition made of the legislative power? By the legislative power's being lodged in the hands of a single person, as in the case of a monarchy? No; but to[1] a disposition made of a new power, which comes in, as it were, in a parenthesis, a new power which we now hear of for the first time, a power which has not, by any description given of it, been distinguished from the legislative, an *executive*.

Difficulty of determining what it is as contradistinct to legislative

5. What then is this same executive power? I doubt our Author would not find it a very easy matter to inform us. 'Why not?' says an objector—'is it not that power which in this country the King has in addition to his share in the legislative?' Be it so: the difficulty for a moment is staved off. But that it is far enough from being solved, a few questions will soon shew us. This power, is it that only which the King really *has*, or is it all that he is said to have? Is it that only which he really has, and which he exercises, or is it that also, which although he be said to have it, he neither does exercise, nor may exercise? Does it include judiciary power or not? If it does, does it include the power of making as well *particular* decisions and orders, as *general*, *permanent*, *spontaneous* regulations of procedure, such as are some of those we see made by judges? Doth it include supreme military power, and that as well in ordinary as in a time of martial law? Doth it include the supreme *fiscal* power;[a] and, in general, that power which, extending as

---

[a] By *fiscal* power I mean that which in this country is exercised by what is called the Board of Treasury.

---

[1] So all editions, though the context properly requires 'by'.

well over the public money as over every other article of public property, may be styled the *dispensatorial?*[b] Doth it include the power of granting patents for inventions, and charters of incorporation? Doth it include the right of making bye-laws in corporations? And is the right of making bye-laws in corporations the superior right to that of conferring the power to make them, or is it that there is an executive power that is superior to a legislative? This *executive* again, doth it include the right of substituting the laws of war to the laws of peace; and *vice versa*, the laws of peace to the laws of war? Doth it include the right of restraining the trade of subjects by treaties with foreign powers? Doth it include the right of delivering over, by virtue of the like treaties, large bodies of subjects to foreign laws?—He that would understand what power is executive and not legislative, and what legislative and not executive, he that would mark out and delineate the different species of constitutional powers, he that would describe either what *is*, or what *ought to be* the constitution of a country, and particularly of this country, let him *think of these things.*[2]

6. In the next place we are told in a parenthesis (it being a matter so plain as to be taken for granted) that 'each of these branches of the Legislature is *independent*,'—yes, '*entirely* independent', of the two others.—Is this then really the case? Those who consider the influence which the King and so many of the Lords have in the election of members of the House of Commons; the power which the

Independence inaccurately attributed to the three branches of the Government

---

[b] By *dispensatorial* power I mean as well that which is exercised by the Board of Treasury, as those others which are executed in the several offices styled with us the War Office, Admiralty Board, Navy Board, Board of Ordnance, and Board of Works: excepting from the business of all these offices, the power of appointing persons to fill other subordinate offices: a power which seems to be of a distinct nature from that of making disposition of any article of public property.

Power, political power, is either over *persons* or over *things*. The powers, then, that have been mentioned above, in as far as they concern *things*, are powers over such *things* as are the property of the public: powers which differ in this from those which constitute private ownership, in that the former are, in the main, not *beneficial* (that is, to the possessors themselves) and *indiscriminate*; but *fiduciary*, and *limited* in their exercise to such *acts* as are conducive to the *special* purposes of *public* benefit and security.[1]

---

[1] Bentham's *Of Laws in General* includes a detailed analysis and clarification of legal powers: cf. esp. op. cit., in *CW*, 21–3, 81–92, 256–71, and 290–6, where the distinctions drawn in this footnote are further developed.

[2] Philippians 4:8: 'Finally, brethren, whatsoever things are true, whatsoever things are just, whatsoever things are pure, whatsoever things are lovely, whatsoever things are of good report; if there be any virtue, and if there be any praise, think on these things.'

King has, at a minute's warning, of putting an end to the existence of any House of Commons; those who consider the influence which the King has over both Houses, by offices of dignity and profit given and taken away again at pleasure; those who consider that the King, on the other hand, depends for his daily bread on both Houses, but more particularly on the House of Commons; not to mention a variety of other circumstances that might be noticed in the same view, will judge what degree of precision there was in our Author's meaning, when he so roundly asserted the affirmative.

A happy discovery—merit inseparable from high station

7. One parenthesis more: for this sentence teems with parenthesis within parenthesis. To this we are indebted for a very interesting piece of intelligence: nothing less than a full and true account of the personal merits of the members of the House of Lords for the time being. This he is enabled to do, by means of a contrivance of his own, no less simple than it is ingenious: to wit, that of looking at their titles. It is by looking at men's titles that he perceives, not merely that they *ought* to possess certain merits, not that there is reason to *wish* they may possess them, but that they do *actually* possess them, and that it is by possessing those merits that they came to possess these titles. Seeing that some are bishops, he knows that they are pious: seeing that some are peers, he knows that they are wise, rich, valiant.[c]

---

[c] 'The Lords spiritual and temporal' (p. 50) 'which', says our Author, '*is* an aristocratical assembly of persons selected for their piety, their birth, their wisdom, their valour, or their property'—[1]
   I have distributed, I think, these endowments, as our Author could not but intend they should be distributed. Birth, to such of the members of that assembly as have their seat in it by *descent*: and, as to those who may chance from time to time to sit there by *creation*, wisdom, valour, and property in *common* among the temporal peers; and piety, singly but entirely, among my Lords the Bishops. As to the other three endowments, if there were any of them to which these right reverend persons could lay any decent claim, it would be wisdom: but since worldly wisdom is what it would be an ill compliment to attribute to them, and the wisdom which is from above[2] is fairly included under piety, I conclude that, when secured in the exclusive possession of this grand virtue, they have all that was intended them. There is a remarkable period in our history, at which, measuring by our Author's scale, these three virtues seem to have been at the boiling point. It was in Queen Anne's reign, not long after the time of the hard frost. I mean in the year 1711. In that auspicious year, these three virtues issued forth, it seems, with such exuberance, as to furnish merit enough to stock no fewer than a dozen respectable persons, who, upon the strength of it, were all made Barons in a day.[3] Unhappily indeed,

---

[1] 1823, no new paragraph here.
[2] James 4:17: 'the wisdom that is from above'.
[3] The Tories came into office under Harley and St John in August 1710. Twelve

8. The more we consider the application he makes of the common-place notions concerning the three forms of Government to our own, the more we shall see the wide difference there is between reading and reflecting. Our own he finds to be a combination of these three. It has a Monarchical branch, an Aristocratical, and a Democratical. The Aristocratical is the House of Lords; the Democratical is the House of Commons. Much had our Author read, at school, doubt-less, and at college, of the wisdom and gravity of the Spartan senate: something, probably, in Montesquieu, and elsewhere, about the Venetian.[3] He had read of the turbulence and extravagance of the Athenian mob. Full of these ideas, the House of Lords were to be our Spartans or Venetians; the House of Commons, our Athenians. With respect then to the point of wisdom, (for that of honesty we will pass by) the consequence is obvious. The House of Commons, however excellent in point of honesty, is an assembly of less *wisdom* than that of the House of Lords. This is what our Author makes no scruple of assuring us. A Duke's son gets a seat in the House of Commons. There needs no more to make him the very model of an Athenian cobbler.

Supposed qualities of the three pretended forms of Government not applicable to our own

9. Let us find out, if we can, whence this notion of the want of so little read was a right reverend and contemporary historian,* in our Author's method of 'discerning of spirits,'[2] as to fancy, it was neither more nor less than the necessity of making a majority that introduced so large a body of new members thus suddenly into the house. But I leave it to those who are read in the history of that time, to judge of the ground there can be for so romantic an imagination. As to piety, the peculiar endowment of the mitre, the stock there is of that virtue, should, to judge by the like standard, be, at all times, pretty much upon a level: at all times, without question, at a *maximum*. This is what we can make the less doubt of, since, with regard to ecclesiastical matters, in general, our Author, as in another place he assures us, has had the happiness to find, that 'every thing is as it should be.'†

Wisdom why likely to be wanting in the members of a Democracy—

* See Bishop Burnet's History of his own Times. Vol. 2.[1]

†Vol. 4. Chap. IV. p. 49.

---

new peers were created in 1711 to counter the opposition of the House of Lords to the new administration's plans for negotiating peace, which ended in the Treaty of Utrecht (1713).

[1] Gilbert Burnet (1643–1715), Bishop of Salisbury from 1689, *The History of My Own Times*, vol. ii (1734), 589.

[2] I Corinthians 12:10.

[3] No extended discussion of the Venetian senate is to be found in such works of Montesquieu as Blackstone could have read. Bentham may have been thinking of *De l'esprit des lois*, II.iii and VIII.v, where Montesquieu advocates a senate chosen for merit from the whole body of the nobility, and speaks of Venice as having corrected the disadvantages inherent in an hereditary aristocracy.

wisdom in the members of a Democracy, and of the abundance of it in those of an Aristocracy, could have had its rise. We shall then see with what degree of propriety such a notion can be transferred to *our* Houses of Lords and Commons.

In the members of a Democracy in particular, there is likely to be a want of wisdom—Why? The greater part being poor, are, when they begin to take upon them the management of affairs, uneducated: being uneducated, they are illiterate: being illiterate, they are ignorant. Ignorant, therefore, and *unwise*, if that be what is meant by ignorant, they *begin*. Depending for their daily bread on the profits of some petty traffic, or the labour of some manual occupation, they are nailed to the work-board, or the counter. In the business of Government, it is only by fits and starts that they have leisure so much as to *act*: they have no leisure to *reflect*. Ignorant therefore they *continue*.— But in what degree is this the case with the members of our House of Commons?

—and present *in those of an Aristocracy*   **10.** On the other hand, the members of an Aristocracy, being few, are rich: either they are members of the Aristocracy, because they are rich; or they are rich, because they are members of the Aristocracy. Being rich, they are educated: being educated, they are learned: being learned, they are knowing. They are at leisure to *reflect*, as well as *act*. They may therefore naturally be expected to become more knowing, that is more wise, as they persevere. In what degree is this the case with the members of the House of Lords more than with those of the House of Commons? The fact is, as every body sees, that either the members of the House of Commons are as much at leisure as those of the House of Lords; or, if occupied, occupied in such a way as tends to give them a more than ordinary insight into some particular department of Government. In whom shall we expect to find so much knowledge of Law as in a professed Lawyer? of Trade, as in a Merchant?

Why, according to our Author   **11.** But hold—Our Author, when he attributes to the members of an Aristocracy more wisdom than to those of a Democracy, has a reason of his own. Let us endeavour to understand it, and then apply it, as we have applied the others. In Aristocratical bodies, we are to understand there is more *experience*; at least it is intended by some body or other there *should be*: which, it seems, answers the same purpose as if there *was*. 'In Aristocracies,' says our Author, 'there is more wisdom to be found, than in the other frames of Government;

being composed,' continues he, 'or intended to be composed, of the most experienced citizens.'[d] On this ground then it is, that we are to take for granted, that the members of the House of Lords have more wisdom among them, than those of the House of Commons. It is this article of *experience* that, being a qualification possessed by the members of an Aristocratical body, as such, in a superior degree to that in which it can be possessed by a democratical body, is to afford us a particular ground for attributing a greater share of wisdom to the members of the upper house, than to those of the lower.

12. How it is that a member of an aristocracy, as such, is, of all things, to have attained more *experience* than the member of a democracy, our Author has not told us; nor what it is this experience is to consist of. Is it experience of things *preparatory* to, but different from, the business of governing? This should rather go by the name of *knowledge*. Is it experience of the business itself of governing? Let us see. For the member of the one body, as of the other, there must be a time when he first enters upon this business. They both enter upon it, suppose on the same day. Now then is it on that same day that one is more experienced in it than the other? or is it on that day ten years? *Superiority of 'experience' how far a proof of superiority of wisdom*

13. Those indeed who recollect what we observed but now,[e] may answer without hesitation,—on that day ten years. The reason was there given. It is neither more nor less, than that want of leisure which the bulk of the numerous members of a Democracy must necessarily labour under, more than those of an Aristocracy. But of this, what intimation is there to be collected, from any thing that has been suggested by our Author? *—how far attributable to aristocracies in general*

14. So much with respect to Aristocracies in general. It happens also by accident, that that particular branch of our *own* government to which he has given the name of the Aristocratical,—the House of Lords,—has actually greater opportunities of acquiring the qualification of experience, than that other branch, the House of Commons, to which he has given the name of the democratical. But to what is this owing? not to any thing in the characteristic natures of those two bodies, not to the one's being Aristocratical, and the other Democratical; but to a circumstance, entirely foreign and accidental, which we shall see presently. But let us observe his reasoning. The *—how far to our House of Lords in particular*

---

[d] p. 50.
[e] V. supra, par. 9.

House of Lords, he says, is an assembly that behoves to have more wisdom in it, than the House of Commons. This is the proposition. Now for the proof. The first is an Aristocratical assembly; the second a Democratical. An Aristocratical assembly has more experience than a Democratical; and on that account more wisdom. Therefore the House of Lords, as was to be proved, has more wisdom than the House of Commons. Now, what the whole of the argument rests upon, we may observe, is this fact, that an Aristocratical assembly, as such, has more experience than a Democratical one; but this, with Aristocratical assemblies in general, we see, is not, for any reason that our Author has given us, the case. At the same time with respect to our House of Lords in particular, in comparison with the House of Commons, it does happen to be the case, owing to this simple circumstance: the members of the House of Lords, when once they begin to sit, sit on for life: those of the House of Commons only from seven years to seven years, or it may happen, less.

What is to be understood by the word 'experience'
15. In speaking, however, in this place, of experience, I would rather be understood to mean opportunity of acquiring experience, than experience itself. For actual experience depends upon other concurrent causes.

Opportunity of experience not the sole course of wisdom
16. It is, however, from superiority of experience alone, that our Author derives superiority of wisdom. He has, indeed, the proverb in his favour: 'Experience,' it has been said of old, 'is the Mother of Wisdom:' be it so;—but then Interest is the Father. There is even an Interest that is the Father of Experience. Among the members of the House of Commons, though none so poor as to be illiterate, are many whose fortunes, according to the common phrase, are yet to make. The fortunes of those of the House of Lords (I speak in general) are made already. The members of the House of Commons may hope to be members of the House of Lords. The members of the House of Lords have no higher House of Lords to rise to. Is it natural for those to be most active who have the *least*, or those who have the *most* interest to be so? Are the experienced those who are the least, or those who are the most active? Does experience come to men when asleep, or when awake? Is it the members of the House of Lords that are the most active, or of the House of Commons? To speak plain, is it in the House of Lords that there is most business done, or in the House of Commons? Was it *after* the *fish* was caught that the successor of St

Peter used the *net*, or was it *before?*[f] In a word is there most wisdom ordinarily where there is least, or where there is most to gain by being wise[g]?[2]

17. A word or two more with respect to the characteristic qualifications, as our Author states them, of the higher assembly of our legislature. Experience is, in virtue of their being an aristocratical assembly, to afford them wisdom: thus far we were arrived before. But he now pushes the deduction a step farther.—Wisdom is to afford them 'circumspection and mediatory caution;' qualifications which it seems as if we should see nothing of, were it not for them. Let us now put a case. The business, indeed, that originates in the House of Lords is, as things stand, so little, that our Author seems to forget that there is any. However, some there is. A bill then originates with the Lords, and is sent down to the Commons.—As to 'circumspection' I say nothing: *that*, let us hope, is not wanting to either House. But whose province is 'mediatory caution,' now?

18. Thus much concerning these two branches of our legislature, so long as they continue what, according to our Author's principles,

Mediatory caution not the peculiar province of the Lords

The Democratical branch of our Legislature, upon our Author's principles, not distinguishable from the Aristocratical

[f] Every body has heard the story of him who, from a fisherman, was made Archbishop, and then Pope. While Archbishop, it was his custom every day, after dinner, to have a fishing net spread upon his table, by way of a memento, as he used to say, of the meanness of his original. This farcical ostentation of humility was what, in those days, contributed not a little to the increase of his reputation. Soon after his exaltation to St Peter's chair, one of his intimates was taking notice to him, one day, when dinner was over, of the table's not being decked as usual. 'Peace', answered the Holy Father, 'when the fish is caught, there is no occasion for the net.'[1]

[g] In the House of Commons itself, is it by the opulent and independent Country gentlemen that the chief business of the House is transacted, or by aspiring, and perhaps needy Courtiers? The man who would persevere in the toil of Government, without any other reward than the favour of the people, is certainly the man for the people to make choice of. But such men are at best but rare. Were it not for those children of Corruption we have been speaking of, the business of the state, I doubt, would stagnate.

---

[1] The original source of this story has not been traced. It is referred to in Samuel Richardson's *Clarissa, or, the History of a Young Lady* (1st edn., v, 1748, 189–90 and n. a). It is doubtful, however, whether Richardson can have been Bentham's immediate source, since there are differences of detail between the two versions. (The story was later used by Robert Browning in his poem 'The Pope and the Net', published in *Asolando*, 1889.) The subject of the anecdote is almost certainly Francesco della Rovere (1414–84), Pope Sixtus IV from 1471. He was born at Celle near Savona on the Ligurian coast, and though he bore a noble name was reputed to have been the son of a fisherman. As cardinal he lived in great austerity and his palace was said to have resembled a monastery.
[2] Dublin, followed by Montague and Harrison, omits the question-mark here.

they are at present: the House of Lords the Aristocratical branch: the House of Commons the Democratical. A little while and we shall see them so; but again a little while, perhaps, and we shall not see them so.[1] By what characteristic does our Author distinguish an Aristocratical legislative body from a Democratical one? By that of *number*: by the number of the persons that compose them: by that, and that alone: for no other has he given. Now, therefore, to judge by that, the House of Lords, at present, indeed, *is* the Aristocratical branch: the House of Commons in comparison at least with the other, the Democratical. Thus far is well. But should the list of nobility swell at the rate we have sometimes seen it, there is an assignable period, and that, perhaps, at no very enormous distance, at which the assembly of the Lords will be more numerous than that of the Commons.[2] Which will *then* be the Aristocratical branch of our Legislature? Upon our Author's principles, the House of Commons. Which the Democratical? The House of Lords.

All perfection of the British Constitution mathematically demonstrated 19. The final cause we are to observe, and finishing exploit, the *'portus et sabbatum'*, as Lord Bacon might perhaps have called it,[h] of this sublime and edifying dissertation, is this demonstration, he has been giving us, of the perfection of the British Form of Government. This demonstration (for by no less a title ought it to be called) is founded, we may have observed, altogether upon the properties of *numbers*: properties, newly discovered indeed, and of an extraordinary complection, *moral* properties; but properties, however, so it seems, of numbers.[i] 'Tis in the nature then of numbers we shall find these characteristic properties of the three Forms of Government, if

---

[h] It is what he says of Theology with respect to the Sciences.—V. Augm. Scient. L. VIII. c. III, p. 97.[3]
[i] V. supra.[4]

---

[1] Cf. John 16:16: 'A little while, and ye shall not see me; and again, a little while, and ye shall see me.'
[2] Though the reign of George III saw a considerable transformation of the House of Lords by new creations, more especially during the long ministry of the younger Pitt, it was not until the twentieth century that the situation envisaged by Bentham here in fact came about.
[3] Bk. VIII. Ch. iii of Bacon's *De Dignitate et Augmentis Scientiarum* (1623) concludes with a description of Theology as 'cunctorum laborum et peregrinationum humanarum Sabbatum et Portum nobilissimum'. Bentham's page-reference does not fit any edition it has been possible to consult: in that of 1645 the passage occurs on p. 729.
[4] The reference is evidently to Ch. II, par. 24, above, citing I Comm. 49.

anywhere. Now the properties of numbers are universally allowed to be the proper subject of that mode of demonstration which is called *mathematical*. The proof our Author has given has therefore already in it the *essence* of such a demonstration. To be compleat at all points, it wants nothing but the *form*. This deficiency is no other than what an under-rate workman might easily supply. A mere technical operation does the business. That humble task it shall be my endeavour to perform. The substantial honour I ascribe wholly to our Author, to whom only it is most due.

20. *PROPOSITION THEOREM*

The demonstration drawn up in form

The British Government is all-perfect

DEMONSTRATION

By definition	1	The British Government = Monarchy + Aristocracy + Democracy.
Again, by definition,	2	Monarchy = the Government of 1.
Also,	3	Democracy = the Government of *all*.
Also,	4	Aristocracy = the Government of some number between 1 and *all*.
Put	5	*All* = 1,000,000.
Put also	6	The number of governors in an Aristocracy = 1000.
Now then, by assumption,	7	1 has + strength — wisdom — honesty.
Also,	8	1000 has + wisdom — strength — honesty.
Also,	9	1,000,000 has + honesty — strength — wisdom.
Rejecting — wisdom — honesty^j in (7)	10	1 has + strength.
Also rejecting — strength — wisdom in (8)	11	1000 has + wisdom.

^{j} Which is done without any sort of ceremony, the quantities marked in the step with the negative sign, being as so many *fluents*,[1] which are at a *maximum*, or a *minimum*, just as happens to be most convenient.

---

[1] In mathematical terminology, fluents are quantities continuously increasing or decreasing by infinitesimal amounts.

Also rejecting — strength — wisdom in (9)	12	1,000,000 has + honesty.
Putting together the expressions (10), (11), and (12),	13	1 + 1000 + 1,000,000 has strength + wisdom + honesty.
But by the definitions (1), (2), (3), (4), and the suppositions (5), (6),	14	The British Government = 1 + 1000 + 1,000,000.
Therefore, by (13)	15	The British Government has + strength + wisdom + honesty.
Changing the expression,	16	The British Government is all-powerful + all-wise + all-honest.
But by definition	17	All-powerful + all-wise + all-honest = all-perfect.
Therefore, by (16) and (17)	18	The British Government is all-perfect, Q. E. D.

☞ SCHOLIUM. After the same manner it may be proved to be *all-weak*, *all-foolish*, and *all-knavish*.

Conclusion of the Chapter

21. Thus much for the British Constitution; and for the grounds of that pre-eminence which it boasts, I trust, indeed, not without reason above all others that are known: Such is the idea our Author gives us of those grounds.—'You are not satisfied with it then', says some one.—Not perfectly.—'What is then your own?'—In truth this is more than I have yet quite settled. I may have settled it with myself, and not think it worth the giving: but if ever I do think it worth the giving, it will hardly be in the form of a comment on a digression stuffed into the belly of a definition. At any rate it is not likely to be much wished for, by those, who have read what has been given us on this subject by an ingenious foreigner: since it is to a foreigner we were destined to owe the best idea that has yet been given of a subject so much our own. Our Author has copied: but Mr. DE L'OLME has thought.[1]

The topic which our Author has thus brought upon the carpet (let any one judge with what necessity) is in respect to some parts of it that we have seen, rather of an invidious nature. Since, however, it *has* been brought upon the carpet, I have treated it with that plainness with which an Englishman of all others is bound to treat it, because an

[1] Jean Louis Delolme (1740–1806) published his *Constitution de l'Angleterre* in 1771.

Englishman may thus treat it and be safe. I have said what the subject seemed to demand, without any fear indeed, but without any wish, to give offence: resolving not to permit myself to consider how this or that man might chance to take it. I have spoken without sycophantical respects indeed, yet I hope not without decency: certainly without any party spleen. I chose rather to leave it to our Author to compliment men in the lump: and to stand aghast with admiration at the virtues of men unknown.[k] Our Author will do as shall seem meet to him. For my part, if ever I stand forth and sing the song of eulogy to great men, it shall be not because they *occupy* their station, but because they *deserve* it.

[k] V. supra, par. 7.

CHAPTER IV
Right of the Supreme Power
to Make Laws

Subject of the
paragraph in
question as stated
by our Author **1.** We now come to the third topic touched upon in the digression; namely, the *right*, as our Author phrases it, which the Supreme Power has of making laws. And this topic occupies one pretty long paragraph. The title here given to it is the same which in the next succeeding paragraph he has found for it himself. This is fortunate: for, to have been obliged to find a title for it myself, is what would have been to the last degree distressing. To *intitle* a discourse, is to represent the drift of it. But, to represent the drift of this, is a task which, so long at least as I confine my consideration to the paragraph itself, bids defiance to my utmost efforts.

Drift of it, as
conjectured **2.** 'Tis to another passage or two, a passage or two that we have already seen starting up in distant parts of this digression, that I am indebted for such conjectures as I have been able to make up.

These conjectures, however, I could not have ventured so far to rely on, as on the strength of them to have furnished the paragraph with a title of my own framing. The danger of misrepresentation was too great; a kind of danger which a man cannot but lie imminently exposed to, who ventures to put a precise meaning upon a discourse which in itself has none. That I may just mention, however, in this place, the result of them; what he is really aiming at, I take it, is, to inculcate a persuasion that in every state there must subsist, in some hands or other, a power that is *absolute*. I mention it thus prematurely, that the reader may have some clue to guide him in his progress through the paragraph; which it is now time I should recite.

The paragraph
recited **3.** 'Having', says our Author, 'thus cursorily considered the three usual species of government, and our own singular constitution,

86

selected and compounded from them all, I proceed to observe, that, as the power of making laws constitutes the supreme authority, so wherever the supreme authority in any state resides, it is the right of that authority to make laws; that is, in the words of our definition, to prescribe the rule of civil action. And this may be discovered from the very end and institution of civil states. For a state is a collective body, composed of a multitude of individuals united for their safety and convenience, and intending to act together as one man. If it therefore is to act as one man, it ought to act by one uniform will. But in as much as political communities are made up of many natural persons, each of whom has his particular will and inclination, these several wills cannot by any *natural* union be joined together, or tempered and disposed into a lasting harmony, so as to constitute and produce that one uniform will of the whole. It can therefore be no otherwise produced than by a *political* union; by the consent of all persons to submit their own private wills to the will of one man, or of one, or more assemblies of men, to whom the supreme authority is entrusted: and this will of that one man, or assemblage of men is, in different states, according to their different constitutions, understood to be law.'[1]

4. The other passages which suggested to me the construction I have ventured to put upon this, shall be mentioned by and by. First, let us try what is to be made of it by itself. *The sense of it considered in itself*

5. The obscurity in which the first sentence of this paragraph is enveloped, is such, that I know not how to go about bringing it to light, without borrowing a word or two of logicians. Laying aside the preamble, the body of it, viz. '*as* the power of making laws constitutes the supreme authority, so where-ever the supreme authority in any state resides, it is the right of that authority to make laws,' may be considered as constituting that sort of syllogism which logicians call an *enthymeme*. An *enthymeme* consists of two *propositions*; a *consequent* and an *antecedent*. 'The power of making laws', says our Author, 'constitutes the supreme authority.' This is his antecedent. From hence it is he concludes, that 'wherever the supreme authority in any state resides, it is the right of that authority to make laws.' This then is his *consequent*. *The leading argument in it nugatory*

---

[1] I Comm. 52: the italics are in the original, where the phrase 'to prescribe the rule of civil action' and the final word 'law' are also italicised, and which reads 'inasmuch' for 'in as much'.

Now so it is, that this *antecedent*, and this *consequent*, for any difference at least that I can possibly perceive in them, would turn out, were they but correctly worded, to mean precisely the same thing: for, after saying that 'the power of making laws constitutes the supreme authority', to tell us that, for that reason, 'the supreme authority' is (or has) the power (or the right) of making laws, is giving us, I take it, much the same sort of information, as it would be to us to be told that a thing is so, *because* it is so: a sort of a truth which there seems to be no very great occasion to send us upon 'discovering, in the end and institution of civil states'. That by the 'sovereign power', he meant 'the power of making laws'; this, or something like it, is no more indeed than what he had told us over and over, and over again, with singular energy and anxiety, in his 46th page, in his 49th, and in, I know not how many, pages besides:[1] always taking care, for precision's sake, to give a little variety to the expression: the words '*power*' and '*authority*', sometimes, seemingly put for the same idea; sometimes seemingly opposed to each other: both of them sometimes denoting the *fictitious* being, the *abstract quality*; sometimes the *real* being or beings, the *person* or *persons* supposed to *possess* that *quality*.— Let us disentangle the sense from these ambiguities; let us learn to speak distinctly of the *persons*, and of the *quality* we attribute to them; and then let us make another effort to find a meaning for this perplexing passage.

The antecedent stated anew 6. By the 'supreme authority' then, (we may suppose our Author to say) 'I mean the same thing as when I say the power of making laws'. This is the proposition we took notice of above, under the name of the *antecedent*. This antecedent then, we may observe, is a definition: a definition, to wit, of the phrase 'supreme authority'. Now to define a phrase is, to translate it into another phrase, supposed to be better understood, and expressive of the same ideas. The supposition here then is, that the reader was already, of himself, tolerably well acquainted with the import of the phrase 'power of making laws': that he was not at all, or was however less acquainted with the import of

---

[1] I Comm. 46: 'Wherefore it is requisite to the very essence of a law, that it be made by the supreme power. Sovereignty and legislature are indeed convertible terms: one cannot subsist without the other.' I Comm. 49: 'By the sovereign power, as was before observed, is meant the making of laws...'. The other passages Bentham had in mind may have included, e.g., I Comm. 147: '...the British parliament; in which the legislative power, and (of course) the supreme and absolute authority of the state, is vested by our constitution.'

the phrase 'supreme authority'. Upon this supposition then, it is, that in order to his being made clearly to understand the latter, he is informed of its being synonymous to the former. Let us now introduce the mention of the *person*: let us add the word '*person*' to the definition; it will be the same definition still in substance, only a little more fully and precisely worded. *For a person to possess* the supreme authority, is *for a person to possess* the power of making laws. This then is what in substance has been already laid down in the *antecedent*.

7. Now let us consider the *consequent*; which, when detached from the context, may be spoken of as making a sentence of itself. 'Wherever', says he, 'the supreme authority in any state resides, it is the *right* of that authority to make Laws'.—By '*wherever*' I take it for granted, he means, '*in whatever persons*': by '*authority*', in the former part of the sentence,—*power*; by the same word, '*authority*', in the latter part of the sentence,—*persons*. Corrected therefore, the sentence will stand thus: *In whatever persons in any state the supreme power resides, it is the right of those persons to make Laws.*

The consequent new stated

8. The only word now remaining undisposed of, is the word '*right*'. And what to think of this, indeed I know not: whether our Author had a meaning in it, or whether he had none. It is inserted, we may observe, in the latter part only of the sentence: it appears not in the former. Concerning this omission, two conjectures here present themselves: it may have happened by accident; or it may have been made by design. If by accident, then the case is, that the idea annexed to the word '*right*' is no other than what was meant to be included in the former part of the sentence, in which it is *not* expressed, as well as in the latter, in which it *is*. In this case it may, without any change in the signification, be expressed in both. Let it then be expressed, and the sentence, take it altogether, will stand thus: *In whatever persons the right of exercising supreme power in any state resides, it is the right of those persons to make Laws.* If this conjecture be the true one, and I am apt to think it is, we see once more, and, I trust, beyond all doubt, that the *consequent* in this *enthymeme* is but a repetition of the *antecedent*. We may judge then, whether it is from any such consideration as that of 'the end and institution of civil states,' or any other consideration that we are likely to gain any further conviction of the truth of this *conclusion*, than it presents us of itself. We may also form some judgment beforehand, what use or meaning there is likely to be in the assemblage of words that is to follow.

That it is identical with the antecedent:

89

—or else nothing to the purpose

9. What is possible, notwithstanding, however improbable, is, that the omission we have been speaking of was *designed*. In this case, what we are to understand is, that the word '*right*' *was* meant to introduce a new idea into this latter part of the sentence, over and above any that was meant to be suggested by the former. '*Right*' then, according to this construction, in the one place, is to be considered as put in contradistinction to *fact* in the other. The sense is then, that *whatever persons* do actually *exercise supreme power*, (or what, according to the *antecedent* of the *enthymeme*, is the same thing, *the power of making laws*) *those persons* have the right to *exercise it*. But, in this case, neither does what is given as a *consequence* in any respect follow from the *antecedent*, nor can *any thing be* made of it, but what is altogether foreign to the rest of the discourse. So much indeed, that it seems more consonant to probability, as well as more favourable to our Author, to conclude that he had no meaning at all, than that he had this.

The rest of the paragraph new stated—supposed drift of it

10. Let us now try what we can make of the remainder of the paragraph. Being ushered in by the word '*for*,' it seems to lay claim to the appellation of an argument. This argument, setting out, as we have seen, without an object, seems however to have found something like one at last, as if it had picked it up by the way. This object, if I mistake it not, is to persuade men, that the *supreme power*, (that is the *person* or *persons* in use to exercise the supreme power in a state) ought, in all points without exception, to be obeyed. What men intend, he says, to do when they are in a state, is to act, as if they were but 'one man.' But one man has but one will belonging to him. What they intend therefore, or what they *ought* to intend, (a slight difference which our Author seems not to be well aware of) is, to act as if they had but one will. To act as if they had but one will, the way is, for them to 'join' all their wills 'together.' To do this, the most obvious way would be to join them '*naturally*:' but, as *wills* will not splice and dovetail like deal boards, the only feasible way is to join them '*politically*.' Now the only way for men to join their wills together *politically*, is for them all to consent to submit their wills to the will of one. This one will, to which all others are to be submitted, is the will of those persons who are in use to exercise the supreme power; whose wills again, when there happens to be many of them, have, by a process of which our Author has said nothing, been reduced (as we must suppose) into *one* already. So far our Author's argument. The above is the substance of it fairly given; not altogether with so much ornament, indeed, as he has given it, but, I trust, with somewhat more precision. The whole concludes, we may observe, with our Author's favourite identical proposition, or something like it, now for the twentieth time repeated.

11. Taking it altogether, it is, without question, a very ingenious argument: nor can any thing in the world answer the purpose better, except just in the case where it happens to be wanted. Not but that a veteran antagonist, trained up in the regular and accustomed discipline of legal fencing, such an one, indeed, *might* contrive perhaps, with due management, to give our Author the honour of the field. But should some undisciplined blunderer, like the Commissary's landlady, thrust in *quart*, when he should have thrust in *tierce*.[1] I doubt much whether he might not get within our Author's *guard.*—I 'intend'?—I 'consent'?—I 'submit' myself?—'Who are you, I wonder, that should know what I do better than I do myself? As to *"submitting my will"* to the wills of the people who made this law you are speaking of,—what I know is, that I never "intended" any such thing: I abominate them, I tell you, and all they ever did, and have always *said* so: and as to my "consent," so far have I been from giving it to their law, that from the first to the last, I have protested against it with all my might.' So much for our refractory disputant.—What I should say to him I know: but what our Author could find to answer to him, is more than I can imagine.[a]

12. Let us now return and pick up those other passages which we supposed to have a respect to the same design that seems to be in view in this. First comes the short introductory paragraph that ushers in the whole digression: a paragraph which, however short, and however

Weakness of it as a persuasive to obedience

A prior paragraph supposed to be relative to the object of this

[a] One thing in the paragraph we are considering is observable; it is the concluding sentence, in which he brings together the ideas of *law* and *will*. Here then, in the tail of a digression, he comes nearer in fact, though without being aware of it, to the giving a just and precise idea of a law, than in any part of the definition itself from whence he is digressing. If, instead of saying that a law is a *will*, he had called it the *expression* of a *will*, and that sort of expression of a will which goes by the name of a *command*, his definition would, so far as this goes, have been clear as well as right. As it is, it is neither the one nor the other. But of this more, if at all, in another place. The definition of law is a matter of too much nicety and importance to be dispatched in a note.

---

[1] In Samuel Foote's comedy *The Commissary* (1765), II.i, the chief character attempts to demonstrate his skill with the sword by fencing with his landlady, Mrs Mechlin, but complains that he is unable to parry her incorrect but effective thrusts: 'Instead of pushing in tierce she pushed me in carte'.

imperfect with respect to the purpose of giving a general view of the contents of those which follow it, was, in despite of method, to expatiate upon this subject. Upon this subject, indeed, he does expatiate with a force of argument and energy of expression which nothing can withstand. 'This', it begins, 'will necessarily lead us into a short enquiry concerning the nature of society and civil government.'[b]—This is all the intimation it gives of the contents of those paragraphs we have examined. Upon *this* before us it touches in energetic terms; but more energetic than precise.—'And the *natural*' (it continues) 'and *inherent* right that belongs to the sovereignty of a state', (*natural* right, observe, that belongs to the sovereignty of a *political* society) 'wherever that sovereignty be lodged, of making and enforcing laws.'[2]

Another   **13.** This is not all. The most emphatical passage is yet behind. It is a passage in that short paragraph[c] which we found to contain such a variety of matter. He is there speaking of the several forms of government now in being. 'However they began', says he, 'or by what right soever they subsist, there *is* and *must be* in all of them a *supreme, irresistible, absolute, uncontrolled* authority, in which the *jura summi imperii*, or the rights of sovereignty, reside.'

Agitation he   **14.** The vehemence, the δεινότς, of this passage is remarkable.
betrays   He ransacks the language: he piles up, one upon another, four of the most tremendous epithets he can find; he heaps Ossa upon Pelion: and, as if the English tongue did not furnish expressions strong or imposing enough, he tops the whole with a piece of formidable Latinity. From all this agitation, it is plain, I think, there is a something which he has very much at heart; which he wishes, but fears, perhaps, to bring out undisguised: which in several places, notwithstanding, bursts out involuntarily, as it were, before he is well ready for it; and which, a certain discretion, getting at last the upper hand of propensity, forces, as we have seen, to dribble away in a string of obscure sophisms. Thus oddly enough it happens, that that passage

---

[b] I Comm. p. 47.[1]
[c] I Comm. p. 48,[3] supra, ch. II. par. 11.

---

[1] Which, however, reads 'naturally' for 'necessarily'.
[2] On this passage from I Comm. 47 see also *Comment on the Commentaries*, I. 7, in *CW*, 58.
[3] More precisely, I Comm. 48–9.

of them all, which, if I mistake not, is the only one that was meant to be dedicated expressly to the subject, is the least explicit on it.[d]

15. A courage much stauncher than our Author's might have wavered here. A task of no less intricacy was here to be travelled through, than that of adjusting the claims of those two jealous antagonists, Liberty and Government. A more invidious ground is scarcely to be found any where within the field of politics. Enemies encompass the traveller on every side. He can scarce stir but he must expect to be assaulted with the war-hoop of political heresy from one quarter or another. Difficult enough is the situation of him, who, in these defiles, feels himself impelled one way by fear, and another by affection. *Cause of it*

16. To return to the paragraph which it was the more immediate business of this chapter to examine:—Were the path of obscurity less familiar to our Author, one should be tempted to imagine he had struck into it on the particular occasion before us, in the view of extricating himself from this dilemma. A discourse thus prudently indeterminate might express enough to keep fair with the rulers of the earth, without setting itself in direct array against the prejudices of the people. Viewed by different persons, it might present different aspects: to men in power it might recommend itself, and that from the first, under the character of a practical lesson of obedience for the use of the people; while among the people themselves it might pass muster, for a time at least, in quality of a string of abstract scientific propositions of jurisprudence. It is not till some occasion for making application of it should occur, that its true use and efficacy would be brought to light. The people, no matter on what occasion, begin to murmur, and concert measures of resistance. Now then is the time for the latent virtues of this passage to be called forth. The book is to be opened to them, and in this passage they are to be shewn, what of themselves, perhaps, they would never have observed, a set of arguments curiously strung together and wrapped up, in proof of the universal expedience, or rather *necessity*, of submission: a necessity which is to arise, not out of the reflection that *the probable mischiefs of resistance are greater than the probable mischiefs of obedience*; not out of any such debateable consideration; but out of a something that is to be much more cogent and effectual: to wit, a certain *metaphysico-legal* *Resource he finds in obscurity*

---

[d] Another passage or two there is which might seem to glance the same way: but these I pass over as less material, after those which we have seen.

impotence, which is to beget in them the sentiment, and answer all the purposes of a natural one. Armed, and full of indignation, our malecontents are making their way to the royal palace. In vain. A certain *estoppel*[1] being made to bolt out upon them, in the manner we have seen, by the force of our Author's legal engineering, their arms are to fall, as it were by enchantment, from their hands. To disagree, to clamour, to oppose, to take back, in short, their wills again, is now, they are told, too late: it is what *can*not be done: their wills have been put in *hotchpot*[2] along with the rest: they *have* 'united',—they *have* 'consented',—they *have* 'submitted'.—Our Author having thus *put his hook into their nose,*[3] they are to go back as they came, and all is peace. An ingenious contrivance this enough: but popular passion is not to be fooled, I doubt, so easily. Now and then, it is true, one error may be driven out, for a time, by an opposite error: one piece of nonsense by another piece of nonsense: but for barring the door effectually and for ever against all error and all nonsense, there is nothing like the simple truth.

Inconsistency of the present passage with a former

17. After all these pains taken to inculcate unreserved submission, would any one have expected to see our Author himself among the most eager to excite men to disobedience? and that, perhaps, upon the most frivolous pretences? in short, upon any pretence whatsoever? Such, however, upon looking back a little, we shall find him. I say, among the most eager; for other men, at least the most enlightened advocates for liberty, are content with leaving it to subjects to resist, for their own sakes, on the footing of *permission*: this will not content our Author, but he must be forcing it upon them as a point of *duty*.

The former passage recited

18. 'Tis in a passage antecedent to the digression we are examining, but in the same section, that, speaking of the pretended law of Nature, and of the law of revelation, 'no human laws', he says, 'should be *suffered* to contradict these'.[e] The expression is remarkable. It is

[e] I Comm. p. 42.[4]

---

[1] An estoppel is a legal bar to a person's right to do or to allege something where this would frustrate expectations to which his own previous act or declaration has given rise and upon which others have acted.

[2] Properties of different persons are said to be put 'into hotch-pot' when they are considered as part of a single fund for certain legal purposes. Thus if a fund is to be divided among a class of persons in certain proportions, a 'hotch pot' clause may direct that advances made before its division to any beneficiaries shall be added to the fund for the purpose of computing the amounts due to each.

[3] Isaiah 37:29.

[4] On this see also *Comment on the Commentaries*, Appendix C, in *CW*, 300.

not that no human laws should contradict them: but that no human laws should be SUFFERED to contradict them. He then proceeds to give us an example. This example, one might think, would be such as should have the effect of softening the dangerous tendency of the rule:—on the contrary, it is such as cannot but enhance it;[f] and, in the application of it to the rule, the substance of the latter is again repeated in still more explicit and energetic terms. 'Nay,' says he, speaking of the act he instances, 'if any human law should allow or enjoin us to commit it, we are BOUND TO TRANSGRESS that human law, or else we must offend both the natural and the divine.'[1]

19. The propriety of this dangerous maxim, so far as the Divine Law is concerned, is what I must refer to a future occasion for more particular consideration.[g] As to the LAW *of Nature*, if (as I trust it will appear) it be nothing but a phrase;[h] if there be no other medium for proving any act to be an offence against it, than the mischievous tendency of such act; if there be no other medium for proving a law of the *state* to be contrary to it, than the *inexpediency* of such law, unless the bare unfounded disapprobation of any one who thinks of it be called a proof; if a test for distinguishing such laws as would be *contrary* to the LAW *of Nature* from such as, *without* being contrary to it, are simply *inexpedient*, be that which neither our Author, nor any man else, so much as pretended ever to give; if, in a word, there be scarce any law whatever but what those who have not liked it have found, on some account or another, to be repugnant to some text of scripture; I see no remedy but that the natural tendency of such doctrine is to

Dangerous tendency of it

[f] It is that of murder. In the word here chosen there lurks a fallacy which makes the proposition the more dangerous as it is the more plausible. It is too important to be altogether past over: at the same time that a slight hint of it, in this place, is all that can be given. Murder is *killing* under certain *circumstances*.—Is the human law then to be allowed to define, in *dernier resort*, what shall be those *circumstances*, or is it not? If yes, the case of a 'human law allowing or enjoining us to commit it,' is a case that is not so much as supposable: if *no*, adieu to all human laws: to the fire with our Statutes at large, our Reports, our Institutes, and all that we have hitherto been used to call our law books; our law books, the only law books we can be safe in trusting to, are Puffendorf and the Bible.

[g] According to our Author, indeed, it should be to no purpose to make any separate mention of the two laws; since the Divine Law, he tells us, is but 'a part of' that of Nature.* Of consequence, with respect to that part, at least, which is common to both, to be contrary to the one, is, of course, to be contrary to the other.

[h] This is what there would be occasion to shew more at large in examining some former parts of this section.

* I Comm. p. 42.

[1] I Comm. 43. On this see also *Comment on the Commentaries*, I.4, in *CW*, 32.

impel a man, by the force of conscience, to rise up in arms against any law whatever that he happens not to like. What sort of government it is that can consist with such a disposition, I must leave to our Author to inform us.

The principle of **UTILITY** *the only guide under these difficulties*

20. It is the principle of *utility*, accurately apprehended and steadily applied, that affords the only clue to guide a man through these straits. It is for that, if any, and for that alone to furnish a decision which neither party shall dare in *theory* to disavow. It is something to reconcile men even in theory. They are at least, *something* nearer to an effectual union, than when at variance as well in respect of theory as of practice.

Juncture for resistance

21. In speaking of the supposed contract between King and people,[i] I have already had occasion to give the description, and, as it appears to me, the only *general* description that *can* be given, of that juncture at which, and not before, resistance to government becomes *commendable*; or, in other words, reconcileable to just notions, whether of *legal* or not, at least of *moral*, and, if there be any difference, *religious* duty.[j] What was there said was spoken, at the time, with reference to that particular branch of government which was then in question; the branch that in this country is administered by the King. But if it was just, as applied to *that* branch of government, and in *this* country, it could only be for the same reason that it is so when applied to the *whole* of government, and that in *any* country whatsoever. It is *then*, we may say, and not till then, allowable to, if not incumbent on, every man, as well on the score of *duty* as of *interest*, to enter into measures of resistance; when, according to the best calculation he is able to make, *the probable mischiefs of resistance* (speaking with respect to the community in general) *appear less to him than the probable mischiefs of submission.* This then is to him, that is to each man in particular, the *juncture for resistance.*

Not characterizable by any common *sign*

22. A natural question here is—by what *sign* shall this juncture be known? By what *common* signal alike conspicuous and perceptible to all? A question which is readily enough started, but to which, I hope, it will be almost as readily perceived that it is impossible to find an answer. *Common* sign for such a purpose, I, for my part, know of none: he must be more than a prophet,[1] I think, that can shew us one. For

[i] Ch. I.   [j] See Ch. V. par. 7, note *c*.

---

[1] Matthew 11:9: 'A prophet? yea, I say unto you, and more than a prophet.'

that which shall serve as a particular sign to each particular person,[1] I have already given one—his own internal persuasion of a balance of *utility* on the side of resistance.

23. Unless such a sign then, which I think impossible, can be shewn, the *field*, if one may say so, of the supreme governor's authority, though not *infinite*, must unavoidably, I think, *unless where limited by express convention*,[k] be allowed to be *indefinite*. Nor can I see any narrower, or other bounds to it, under this constitution, or under any other yet *freer* constitution, if there be one, than under the most *despotic*. *Before* the juncture I have been describing were arrived, resistance, even in a country like this, would come too soon: were the juncture arrived *already*, the time for resistance would be come already, under such a government even as any one should call *despotic*.

Freedom in a government depends not upon any limitation to the Supreme Power

24. In regard to a government that is *free*, and one that is *despotic*, wherein is it then that the difference consists? Is it that those persons in whose hands that power is lodged which is acknowledged to be supreme, have less power in the one than in the other, when it is from custom that they derive it? By no means. It is not that the power of one any more than of the other has any certain bounds to it. The distinction turns upon circumstances of a very different complexion:—on the *manner* in which that whole mass of power, which, taken together, is supreme, is, in a free state, *distributed* among the several ranks of persons that are sharers in it:—on the *source* from whence their titles to it are successively derived:—on the frequent and easy *changes* of condition between gover*nors* and gover*ned*; whereby the interests of the one class are more or less indistinguishably blended with those of the other:—on the *responsibility* of the governors; or the right which a subject has of having the reasons publicly assigned and canvassed of every act of power that is exerted over him:—on the *liberty of the press*; or the security with which every man, be he of the one class or the other, may make known his

Principal circumstances on which it does depend

---

[k] This respects the case where one state has, upon *terms*, submitted itself to the government of another: or where the governing bodies of a number of states agree to take directions in certain specified cases, from some *body* or other that is distinct from all of them: consisting of members, for instance, appointed out of each.

---

[1] Dublin here reads, 'For that which shall serve as a particular person...'. Montague, followed by Harrison, emends this by deleting 'as' – an emendation which is the clearest evidence that the Montague text is based on Dublin, not 1776, where (as also in 1823) the text reads correctly as above. Bowring also has the correct reading.

complaints and remonstrances to the whole community:—on the *liberty of public association*; or the security with which malecontents may communicate their sentiments, concert their plans, and practise every mode of opposition short of actual revolt, before the executive power can be legally justified in disturbing them.

Freedom in a government—how far favourable to resistance

25. True then, it may be, that, owing to this last circumstance in particular, in a state thus circumstanced, the road to a revolution, if a revolution be necessary, is to appearance shorter; certainly more smooth and easy. More likelihood, certainly there is of its being such a revolution as shall be the work of a number; and in which, therefore, the interests of a number are likely to be consulted. Grant then, that by reason of these facilitating circumstances, the juncture itself may arrive sooner, and upon less provocation, under what is called a *free* government, than under what is called an *absolute* one: grant this;— yet till it *be* arrived, resistance is as much too soon under one of them as under the other.

The supreme power not limited in itself

26. Let us avow then, in short, steadily but calmly, what our Author hazards with anxiety and agitation, that the authority of the supreme body cannot, *unless where limited by express convention*, be said to have any assignable, any certain bounds.—That to say there is any act they *cannot* do,—to speak of any thing of their's as being *illegal*,—as being *void*;—to speak of their exceeding their *authority* (whatever be the phrase)—their *power*, their *right*,—is, however common, an abuse of language.

Arguments that suppose it to be so, unsatisfactory—

27. The legislature *can*not do it? The legislature *can*not make a law to this effect? Why cannot? What is there that should hinder them? Why not this, as well as so many other laws murmured at, perhaps, as inexpedient, yet submitted to without any question of the *right*? With men of the same party, with men whose affections are already listed[1] against the law in question, any thing will go down: any rubbish is good that will add fuel to the flame. But with regard to an impartial by-stander, it is plain that it is not denying the right of the legislature, their *authority*, their *power*, or whatever be the word—it is not denying that they *can* do what is in question—it is not that, I say, or any discourse verging that way that can tend to give *him* the smallest satisfaction.

—and inapplicable to particulars

28. Grant even the proposition in general:—What are we the nearer? Grant that there *are* certain bounds to the *authority* of the

---

[1] Montague, followed by Harrison, 'lifted'.

legislature:—Of what use is it to say so, when these bounds are what nobody[1] has ever attempted to mark out to any useful purpose; that is, in any such manner whereby it might be known beforehand what description a law must be of to fall *within*, and what to fall *beyond* them? Grant that there *are* things which the legislature *can*not do;—grant that there *are* laws which exceed the *power* of the legislature to establish. What rule does this sort of discourse furnish us for determining whether any one that is in question is, or is not of the number? As far as I can discover, none. Either the discourse goes on in the confusion it began;—either all rests in vague assertions, and no intelligible argument at all is offered, or if any, such arguments as are drawn from the principle of *utility*: arguments which, in whatever variety of words expressed, come at last to neither more nor less than this; that the tendency of the law is, to a greater or a less degree, pernicious. If this then be the result of the argument, why not come home to it at once? Why turn aside into a wilderness of sophistry, when the path of plain reason is straight[2] before us?

29. What practical inferences those who maintain this language mean should be deduced from it, is not altogether clear; nor, perhaps, does every one mean the same. Some who speak of a law as being *void* (for to this expression, not to travel through the whole list, I shall confine myself) would persuade us to look upon the authors of it as having thereby *forfeited*, as the phrase is, their *whole* power: as well that of giving force to the particular law in question, as to any other. These are they who, had they arrived at the same practical conclusion through the principle of utility, would have spoken of the law as being to such a degree pernicious, as that, were the bulk of the community to see it in its true light, *the probable mischief of resisting it would be less than the probable mischief of submitting to it.* These point, in the first instance, at *hostile* opposition. *What they lead to is either an appeal to the body of the people—*

30. Those who say nothing about forfeiture are commonly less violent in their views. These are they who, were they to ground themselves on the principle of utility, and, to use our language, would have spoken of the law as being mischievous indeed, but without speaking of it as being mischievous to the degree that has been just mentioned. The mode of opposition which they point to is one which passes under the appellation of a *legal* one. *—or to the judicial power*

---

[1] Dublin, followed by Montague and Harrison, 'no body'.
[2] So spelt 1823; 1776 (and Dublin) 'streight'.

Which tends to give it a control over the legislative

31. Admit then the law to be void in their sense, and mark the consequences. The idea annexed to the epithet *void* is obtained from those instances in which we see it applied to a private instrument. The consequence of a *private* instrument's being void is, that all persons concerned are to act as if no such instrument had existed. The consequence, accordingly, of a *law's* being void must be, that people shall act as if there were no such law about the matter: and therefore that if any person in virtue of the mandate of the law should do anything in coercion of another person, which without such law he would be punishable for doing, he would still be punishable; to wit, by appointment of the judicial power. Let the law for instance, be a law imposing a tax: a man who should go about to levy the tax by force would be punishable as a trespasser: should he chance to be killed in the attempt, the person killing him would *not* be punishable as for murder: should he kill, he himself *would*, perhaps, be punishable as for murder. To whose office does it appertain to do those acts in virtue of which such punishment would be inflicted? To that of the Judges. Applied to practice then, the effect of this language is, by an appeal made to the Judges, to confer on those magistrates a controlling power over the acts of the legislature.

—A remedy worse than the disease

32. By this management a *particular* purpose might perhaps, by chance be answered: and let this be supposed a good one. Still what benefit would, from the *general* tendency of such a doctrine, and such a practice in conformity to it, accrue to the body of the people is more than I can conceive. A Parliament, let it be supposed, is too much under the influence of the Crown: pays too little regard to the sentiments and the interests of the people. Be it so. The people at any rate, if not so great a share as they might and ought to have, have had, at least, *some* share in chusing it. Give to the Judges a power of annulling its acts; and you transfer a portion of the supreme power from an assembly which the people have had *some* share, at least, in chusing, to a set of men in the choice of whom they have not the least imaginable share; to a set of men appointed solely by the Crown: appointed *solely*, and avowedly and *constantly*, by that very magistrate whose partial and occasional influence is the very grievance you seek to remedy.

But not so bad as some might represent it

33. In the heat of debate, some, perhaps, would be for saying of this management that it was transferring at once the supreme authority from the legislative power to the judicial. But this would be going too

100

far on the other side. There is a wide difference between a *positive* and a *negative* part in legislation. There is a wide difference again between a negative upon *reasons* given, and a negative without any. The power of *repealing* a law even for reasons given is a great power: too great indeed for Judges: but still very distinguishable from, and much inferior to that of *making* one.[1]

34. Let us now go back a little. In denying the existence of any assignable bounds to the supreme power, I added,[m] 'unless where limited by express convention': for this exception I could not but subjoin. Our Author indeed, in that passage in which, short as it is, he is the most explicit, leaves, we may observe, no room for it. 'However they began', says he (speaking of the several forms of government) 'however they began, and by what right soever they subsist, there is and must be in ALL of them an authority that is absolute.' ...[1] To say this, however, of *all* governments without exception;—to say that *no* assemblage of men can subsist in a state of government, without being subject to some *one* body whose authority stands unlimited so much as by convention; to say, in short, that not even by convention can any limitation be made to the power of that body in a state which in other respects is supreme, would be saying, I take it, rather too much: it would be saying that there is no such thing as government in the German Empire; nor in the Dutch Provinces; nor in the Swiss Cantons; nor was of old in the Achaean league.[2]

The supreme power limitable by convention

35. In this mode of limitation I see not what there is that need surprize us. By what is it that any degree of *power* (meaning *political power*) is established? It is neither more nor less, as we have already had occasion to observe,[n] than a habit of, and disposition to

—So as the term of it be explicit

[f] Notwithstanding what has been said, it would be in vain to dissemble, but that, upon occasion, an appeal of this sort may very well answer. and has, indeed, in general, a tendency to answer, in some sort, the purposes of those who espouse, or profess to espouse, the interests of the people. A public and authorized debate on the propriety of the law is by this means brought on. The artillery of the tongue is played off against the law, under cover of the law itself. An opportunity is gained of impressing sentiments unfavourable to it, upon a numerous and attentive audience. As to any other effects from such an appeal, let us believe that in the instances in which we have seen it made, it is the certainty of miscarriage that has been the encouragement to the attempt.

[m] V. supra, par. 26.   [n] V. supra, ch. I. par. 13, note o.

_____

[1] Dublin, followed by Montague and Harrison, substitutes a dash for the dots used at this point in 1776 (and 1823).

[2] All the political systems cited here were instances of a federal distribution of powers.

obedience: *habit*, speaking with respect to *past* acts; *disposition*, with respect to *future*. This disposition it is as easy, or I am much mistaken, to conceive as being absent with regard to one sort of acts; as present with regard to another.[2] For a body then, which is in other respects supreme, to be conceived as being with respect to a certain sort of acts, limited, all that is necessary is, that this sort of acts be in its description distinguishable from every other.

Which furnishes what may be taken for a common signal of resistance
    36. By means of a convention then we are furnished with that common signal which, in other cases, we despaired of finding.[o] A certain act is in the instrument of convention specified, with respect to which the government is therein precluded from issuing a law to a certain effect: whether to the effect of commanding the act, of permitting it, or of forbidding it. A law is issued to that effect notwithstanding. The issuing then of such a law (the sense of it, and likewise the sense of that part of the convention which provides against it being supposed clear) is a fact notorious and visible to all: in the issuing then of such a law we have a fact which is *capable* of being taken for that common signal we have been speaking of. These bounds the supreme body in question has marked out to its authority: of such a demarcation then what is the effect? either none at all, or this: that the disposition to obedience confines itself within these bounds. Beyond them the disposition is stopped from extending: beyond them the subject is no more prepared to obey the governing body of his own state, than that of any other. What difficulty, I say, there should be in conceiving a state of things to subsist in which the supreme authority is thus limited,—what greater difficulty in conceiving it with this limitation, than without any, I cannot see. The two states are, I must confess, to me alike conceivable: whether alike expedient,—alike conducive to the happiness of the people, is another question.

A salvo for reformation
    37. God forbid, that from any thing here said it should be concluded that in any society any convention is or can be made, which shall have the effect of setting up an insuperable bar to that which the parties affected shall deem a reformation:—God forbid that any disease in the constitution of a state should be without its remedy.

[o] V. supra, par. 22.

---

[2] Montague, followed by Harrison, mistakenly reads 'other'.

Such might by some be thought to be the case, where that supreme body which in such a convention, was one of the contracting parties, having incorporated itself with that which was the other, no longer subsists to give any new modification to the engagement. Many ways might however be found to make the requisite alteration, without any departure from the spirit of the engagement. Although that body itself which contracted the engagement be no more, a *larger body*, from whence the first is understood to have derived its title, may still subsist. Let this larger body be consulted. Various are the ways that might be conceived of doing this, and that without any disparagement to the dignity of the subsisting legislature: of doing it, I mean to such effect, as that, should the sense of such *larger body* be favourable to the alteration, it may be made by a law, which, in this case, neither ought to be, nor probably would be, regarded by the body of the people as a breach of the convention.[P]

38. To return for a moment to the language used by those who speak of the supreme power as being limited in its own nature. One thing I would wish to have remembered. What is here said of the impropriety, and evil influence of that kind of discourse, is not intended to convey the smallest censure on those who use it, as if intentionally accessary to the ill effects it has a tendency to produce. It is rather a misfortune in the language, than a fault of any person in

Notion of a natural limit to the supreme power, difficult to eradicate

---

[P] In Great Britain, for instance, suppose it were deemed necessary to make an alteration in the Act of Union. If in an article stipulated in favour of England, there need be no difficulty; so that there were a majority for the alteration among the English members, without reckoning the Scotch. The only difficulty would be with respect to an article stipulated in favour of Scotland; on account, to wit, of the small number of the Scotch members, in comparison with the English. In such a case, it would be highly expedient, to say no more, for the sake of preserving the public faith, and to avoid irritating the body of the nation, to take some method for making the establishment of the new law, depend upon their sentiments. One such method might be as follows. Let the new law in question be enacted in the common form. But let its commencement be deferred to a distant period, suppose a year or two: let it then, at the end of that period, be in force, unless petitioned against, by persons of such a description, and in such a number as might be supposed fairly to represent the sentiments of the people in general: persons, for instance, of the description of those who at the time of the Union, constituted the body of electors. To put the validity of the law out of dispute, it would be necessary the fact upon which it was made ultimately to depend, should be in its nature too notorious to be controverted. To determine therefore, whether the conditions upon which the invalidation of it was made to depend, had been complied with, is what must be left to the simple declaration of some person or persons; for instance the King. I offer this only as a general idea: and as one amongst many that perhaps might be offered in the same view. It will not be expected that I should here answer objections, or enter into details.

particular. The original of it is lost in the darkness of antiquity. We inherited it from our fathers, and, maugre all its inconveniences,[1] are likely, I doubt, to transmit it to our children.

This is not a mere affair of words

39. I cannot look upon this as a mere dispute of words. I cannot help persuading myself, that the disputes between contending parties—between the defenders of a law and the opposers of it, would stand a much better chance of being adjusted than at present were they but explicitly and constantly referred at once to the principle of UTILITY. The footing on which this principle rests every dispute, is that of matter of fact; that is, future fact—the probability of certain future contingencies. Were the debate then conducted under the auspices of this principle, one of two things would happen: either men would come to an agreement concerning that probability, or they would see at length, after due discussion of the real grounds of the dispute, that no agreement was to be hoped for. They would at any rate see clearly and explicitly, the point on which the *dis*agreement turned. The discontented party would then take their resolution to resist or to submit, upon just grounds, according as it should appear to them worth their while—according to what should appear to them, the importance of the matter in dispute—according to what should appear to them the probability or improbability of success—*according*, in short, *as the mischiefs of submission should appear to bear a less, or a greater ratio to the mischiefs of resistance.* But the door to reconcilement would be much more open, when they saw that it might be not a mere affair of passion, but a difference of judgment, and that, for any thing they could know to the contrary, a sincere one, that was the ground of quarrel.

The above notion perpetuates wrangling

40. All else is but womanish scolding and childish altercation, which is sure to irritate, and which never can persuade.—'*I* say, the legislature can*not* do this—*I* say, that it *can*. *I* say, that to do this, *exceeds* the bounds of its *authority*—*I* say, it does *not*.'—It is evident, that a pair of disputants setting out in this manner, may go on irritating and perplexing one another for everlasting, without the smallest chance of ever coming to an agreement. It is no more than announcing, and that in an obscure and at the same time, a peremptory and captious manner, their opposite persuasions, or rather affections, on a question of which neither of them sets himself

---

[1] Dublin, followed by Montague and Harrison, 'inconveniencies'.

to discuss the grounds. The question of utility, all this while, most probably, is never so much as at all brought upon the carpet: if it be, the language in which it is discussed is sure to be warped and clouded to make it match with the obscure and entangled pattern, we have seen.

41. On the other hand, had the debate been originally and avowedly instituted on the footing of utility, the parties might at length have come to an agreement; or at least to a visible and explicit issue.— '*I* say, that the mischiefs of the measure in question are to *such* an amount.—*I* say, *not* so, but to a *less*.—*I* say, the benefits of it are only to *such* an amount.—*I* say, *not* so, but to a *greater*.'—This, we see, is a ground of controversy very different from the former. The question is now manifestly a question of conjecture concerning so many future contingent matters of fact: to solve it, both parties then are naturally directed to support their respective persuasions by the only evidence the nature of the case admits of;—the evidence of such *past* matters of fact as appear to be analogous to those contingent *future* ones. Now these *past* facts are almost always numerous: so numerous, that till brought into view for the purpose of the debate, a great proportion of them are what may very fairly have escaped the observation of one of the parties: and it is owing, perhaps, to this and nothing else, that that party is of the persuasion which sets it at variance with the other. Here, then, we have a plain and open road, perhaps, to present reconcilement: at the worst to an intelligible and explicit issue,—that is, to such a ground of difference as may, when thoroughly trodden and explored, be found to lead on to reconcilement at the last. Men, let them but once clearly understand one another, will not be long ere they agree. It is the perplexity of ambiguous and sophistical discourse that, while it distracts and eludes the apprehension, stimulates and inflames the passions.

But it is now high time we should return to our Author, from whose text we have been insensibly led astray, by the nicety and intricacy of the question it seemed to offer to our view.

The principle of UTILITY *puts an end to it*

CHAPTER V
Duty of the Supreme Power to Make Laws

1. We now come to the last topic touched upon in this digression: a certain '*duty*', which, according to our Author's account, the supreme power lies under:—the *duty of making laws*.

2. 'Thus far', says he, 'as to the *right* of the supreme power to make laws; but farther, it is its *duty* likewise. *For since* the respective members are bound to conform themselves to the will of the state, it is expedient that they *receive directions* from the state declaratory of that its will. *But since* it is impossible, in so great a multitude, to give injunctions to every particular man, relative to each particular action, therefore the state establishes general rules for the perpetual information and direction of all persons, in all points, whether of positive or negative duty. And this, in order that every man may know what to look upon as his own, what as another's; what absolute and what relative duties are required at his hands; what is to be esteemed honest, dishonest, or indifferent; what degree every man retains of his natural liberty; what he has given up as the price of the benefits of society; and after what manner each person is to moderate the use and exercise of those rights which the state assigns him, in order to promote and secure the public tranquillity.'[1]

3. Still as obscure, still as ambiguous as ever. The '*supreme power*' we may remember, according to the definition so lately given of it by our Author, and so often spoken of, is neither more nor less than the *power to make laws*. Of this power we are now told that it is its '*duty*' to make laws. Hence we learn—what?—that it is its '*duty*' to do what it

---

[1] I Comm. 52–3, where, however, the beginning of the third sentence quoted reads 'But, as...' for 'But since...'

does; to be, in short, what it is. This then is what the paragraph now before us, with its apparatus of '*fors*', and '*buts*', and '*sinces*', is designed to prove to us. Of this stamp is that meaning, at least, of the initial sentence, which is apparent upon the face of it.

4. Compleat the sense of the phrase, '*to make laws*'; add to it, in this place, what it wants in order to be an adequate expression of the import which the preceding paragraph seemed to annex to it; you have now, for what is mentioned as the object of the '*duty*', another sense indeed, but a sense still more untenable than the foregoing. 'Thus far', says our Author (recapitulating what he had been saying before) 'as to the *right* of the supreme power to make laws.'—By this '*right*' we saw, in the preceding chapter, was meant, a right to make laws *in all cases whatsoever*. 'But further', he now adds, 'it is its *duty* likewise.' Its *duty* then to do—what? to do the same thing that it was before asserted to be its *right* to do—to make laws in all cases whatsoever: or (to use another word, and that our Author's own, and that applied to the same purpose) that it is its duty to be '*absolute*.'[a] A sort of duty this which will probably be thought rather a singular one. *The next most obvious extravagant*

5. Mean time the observation which, if I conjecture right, he really had in view to make, is one which seems very just indeed, and of no mean importance, but which is very obscurely expressed, and not very obviously connected with the purpose[2] of what goes before. The duty he here means is a duty, which respects, I take it, not so much the actual *making* of laws, as the taking of proper measures to *spread abroad* the knowledge of whatever laws happen to *have been* made: a duty which (to adopt some of our Author's own words) is conversant, not so much about *issuing* 'directions', as about providing that such as *are* issued shall be '*received*'. *A third sense proposed*

6. Mean time to speak of the *duties* of a supreme power;—of a *legislature*, meaning a *supreme* legislature;—of a set of men acknowledged to be absolute;—is what, I must own, I am not very fond of. Not that I would wish the subordinate part of the community to be a whit[3] less watchful over their governors, or more disposed to *Objection to the use of the word 'duty' on this occasion*

<hr />

[a] I Comm. p. 49.[1]

<hr />

[1] '... there is and must be in all [forms of government] a supreme, irresistible, absolute, uncontrolled authority ...'

[2] Dublin, followed by Montague and Harrison, 'purport'.

[3] 1776 (and Dublin), 'awhit'; 1823 as above.

unlimited submission in point of *conduct*, than if I were to talk with ever so much peremptoriness of the '*duties*' of these latter, and of the *rights* which the former have against them:[b] what I am afraid of is, running into solecism and confusion in *discourse*.

[b] With this note let no man trouble himself who is not used, or does not intend to use himself, to what are called *metaphysical* speculations: in whose estimation the benefit of understanding clearly what he is speaking of, is not worth the labour.

1. Duty (political)

1. That may be said to be my *duty* to do (understand political duty) which you (or some other person or persons) have a *right* to have me made to do. I then have a DUTY *towards* you: you have a RIGHT as *against* me.

2. Right (political)

2. What you have a right to have me made to do (understand a political right) is that which I am liable, according to law, upon a requisition made on your behalf, to be *punished* for not doing.

3. Punishment a fundamental idea

3. I say *punished*: for without the notion of punishment (that is of *pain* annexed to an act, and accruing on a certain *account*, and from a certain *source*) no notion can we have of either *right* or *duty*.

4. To define or expound

4. Now the idea belonging to the word *pain* is a simple one. To *define* or rather (to speak more generally) to *expound* a word, is to resolve, or to make a progress towards resolving, the idea belonging to it into simple ones.

5. Words not to be expounded but by paraphrasis

5. For expounding the words *duty, right, power, title*, and those other terms of the same stamp that abound so much in ethics and jurisprudence, either I am much deceived, or the only method by which any instruction can be conveyed, is that which is here exemplified. An exposition framed after this method I would term *paraphrasis*.

6. Paraphrasis what

6. A word may be said to be expounded by *paraphrasis*,[1] when not that *word* alone is translated into other *words*, but some whole *sentence* of which it forms a part is translated into another *sentence*; the words of which latter are expressive of such ideas as are *simple*, or are more immediately resolvable into simple ones than those of the former. Such are those expressive of *substances* and *simple modes*, in respect of such *abstract* terms as are expressive of what LOCKE has called *mixed modes*.[2] This, in short, is the only method in which any abstract terms can, at the long run, be expounded to any instructive purpose: that is in terms calculated to raise *images* either of *substances* perceived, or of *emotions*;—sources, one or other of which every idea must be drawn from, to be a clear one.

7. Definition per genus et differentiam, *not universally applicable*

7. The common method of defining—the method *per genus et differentiam*, as logicians call it, will, in many cases, not at all answer the purpose. Among abstract terms we soon come to such as have no *superior genus*. A definition, *per genus et differentiam*,

---

[1] For a further account of paraphrasis as a method of exposition of the meaning of certain words such as those cited here, which according to Bentham were not susceptible of definition by 'the common method of defining', see Bowring, viii, 126–7, 246–8; also *Of Laws in General*, in *CW*, 224–5.

[2] *Essay concerning Human Understanding*, II.xii and xxii.

7. I understand, I think, pretty well, what is meant by the word *duty* (political duty) when applied to myself; and I could not persuade myself, I think, to apply it in the same sense in a regular didactic discourse to those whom I am speaking of as my supreme governors. That is my *duty* to do, which I am liable to be *punished*, according to law, if I do not do: this is the original, ordinary, and proper sense of the word *duty*.^c Have these supreme governors any such duty? No: for

The proper *sense of it*

when applied to these, it is manifest, can make no advance: it must either stop short, or turn back, as it were, upon itself, in a *circulate* or a *repetend*.[1]

8. 'Fortitude is a virtue;'—Very well:—but what is a virtue? 'A virtue is a disposition:'—Good again:—but what is a *disposition*? 'A *disposition* is a...;' and there we stop. The fact is, a *disposition* has no *superior genus*: a *disposition* is not a ...., any thing:—this is not the way to give us any notion of what is meant by it. 'A *power*,' again 'is a *right*:' and what is a *right*? It is a *power*.—An *estate* is an *interest*, says our Author somewhere; where he begins defining an estate:[2]—as well might he have said an *interest* was an *estate*. As well, in short, were it to define in this manner, a conjunction or a preposition. As well were it to say of the preposition *through*, or the conjunction *because*; a *through* is a ..., or a *because* is a ...., and so go on defining them.

8. Further examples;— disposition,— estate,— interest,—power

9. Of this stamp, by the bye, are some of his most fundamental definitions: of consequence they must leave the reader where they found him. But of this, perhaps, more fully, and methodically on some future occasion. In the meantime I have thrown out these loose hints for the consideration of the curious.

9. An imperfection frequent in our Author's method

1. One may conceive three sorts of duties: *political*, *moral*, and *religious*; correspondent to the three sorts of *sanctions* by which they are enforced: or the same point of conduct may be a man's duty on these three several accounts. After speaking of the one of these to put the change upon the reader, and without warning begin speaking of another, or not to let it be seen from the first which of them one is speaking of, cannot but be productive of confusion.

1. Duties three sorts

2. Political duty is created by punishment; or at least by the will of persons who have punishment in their hands; persons stated and *certain*,—political superiors.

2. Political duty

3. Religious duty is also created by punishment: by punishment expected at the hands of a person *certain*,—the Supreme Being.

3. Religious duty

4. Moral duty is created by a kind of motive, which from the *uncertainty* of the *persons* to apply it, and of the *species* and *degree* in which it will be applied, has hardly yet got the name of punishment: by various mortifications resulting from the ill-will of

4. Moral duty

---

[1] In mathematical terminology, a circulate is a recurring decimal, while the repetend is that part of it which recurs. Dublin, followed by Montague and Harrison, has the meaningless reading 'repented'. 1823 and Bowring have the correct 1776 reading.

[2] II Comm. 103: 'An estate in lands, tenements, and hereditaments, signifies such interest as the tenant hath therein...'

if they are at all liable to punishment according to law, whether it be for *not* doing any thing, or for *doing*, then are they not, what they are supposed to be, supreme governors:[d] those are the supreme gov-

persons *un*certain and variable,—the community in general: that is, such individuals of that community as he, whose duty is in question, shall happen to be connected with.

5. Difference between these senses and a fourth which is figurative and improper

5. When in any of these three senses a man asserts a point of conduct to be a duty, what he asserts is the existence, actual or probable, of an *external* event: viz. of a punishment issuing from one or other of these sources in consequence of a contravention of the duty: an event *extrinsic* to, and distinct from, as well the conduct of the party spoken of, as the sentiment of him who speaks. If he persists in asserting it to be a duty, but without meaning it should be understood that it is on any one of these three accounts that he looks upon it as such; all he then asserts is his own internal *sentiment*: all he means then is, that he feels himself *pleased* or *displeased* at the thoughts of the point of conduct in question, but without being able to tell *why*. In this case he should e'en say so: and not seek to give an undue influence to his own single suffrage, by delivering it in terms that purport to declare the voice either of God, or of the law, or of the people.

6. Duty not applicable here in any proper *sense*

6. Now which of all these senses of the word our Author had in mind; in which of them all he meant to assert that it was the duty of supreme governors to make laws, I know not. *Political* duty is what they cannot be subject to:* and to say that a duty even of the *moral* or *religious* kind to this effect is incumbent on them, seems rather a precipitate assertion.

In truth what he meant was neither more nor less, I suppose, than that he should be glad to see them do what he is speaking of; to wit, '*make* laws:' that is, as he explains himself, spread abroad the knowledge of them. Would he so? So indeed should I; and if asked why, what answer our Author would give I know not; but I, for my part, have no difficulty. I answer,—because I am persuaded that it is for the benefit of the community that they (its governors) should do so. This would be enough to warrant me in my own opinion for saying that they *ought* to do it. For all this, I should not at any rate say that it was their *duty* in a *political* sense. No more should I venture to say it was in a *moral* or *religious* sense, till I were satisfied whether they themselves *thought* the measures useful and feasible, and whether they were generally *supposed* to think so.

Were I satisfied that they *themselves* thought so, God then, I might say, knows they do. God, we are to suppose, will punish them if they neglect pursuing it. It is then their *religious* duty. Were I satisfied that the *people* supposed they thought so: the people, I might say, in case of such neglect,—the people, by various manifestations of its ill-will, will also punish them. It is then their *moral* duty.

In any of these senses it must be observed, there can be no more propriety in averring it to be the duty of the supreme power to pursue the measure in question, than in averring it to be their duty to pursue any other supposable measure equally beneficial to the community. To usher in the proposal of a measure in this peremptory and assuming guise, may be pardonable in a loose rhetorical harangue, but can never be justifiable in an exact didactic composition. Modes of *private moral* conduct there are

Governors in what way subject to political duties notwithstanding d their being supreme

indeed many, the tendency whereof is so well known and so generally acknowledged, that the observance of them may well be stiled a duty. But to apply the same term to the particular details of *legislative* conduct, especially newly proposed ones, is going, I think, too far, and tends only to confusion.

I mean for what they do, or omit to do, when *acting in a body*: in that body in which, when

* See the note following.

110

ernors, by whose appointment the former are liable to be punished.

8. The word duty, then, if applied to persons spoken of as supreme governors, is evidently applied to them in a sense which is figurative and improper: nor therefore are the same conclusions to be drawn from any propositions in which it is used in this sense, as might be drawn from them if it were used in the other sense, which is its proper one.

That in which it is here used figurative

9. This explanation, then, being premised;—understanding myself to be using the word *duty* in its improper sense, the proposition that it is the duty of the legislature to spread abroad, as much as possible, the knowledge of their will among the people, is a proposition I am disposed most unreservedly to accede to. If this be our Author's meaning, I join myself to him heart and voice.

The proposition acceded to in this last sense

10. What particular institutions our Author wished to see established in this view—what *particular* duties he would have found for the legislature under this *general* head of duty, is not very apparent; though it is what should have appeared more precisely than it does, ere his meaning could be apprehended to any purpose. What encreases still the difficulty of apprehending it, is a practice which we have already had more than once occasion to detect him in,[e]—a kind of versatility, than which nothing can be more vexatious to a reader who makes a point of entering into the sentiments of his Author. He sets out with the word '*duty*' in his mouth; and, in the character of a *Censor*, with all due gravity begins talking to us of what *ought* to be. 'Tis in the midst of this lecture that our *Proteus* slips aside; puts on the *historian*; gives an insensible turn to the discourse; and, without any warning of the change, finishes with telling us what *is*. Between these two points, indeed, the *is*, and the *ought to be*, so opposite as they frequently are in the eyes of other men, that spirit of obsequious *quietism* that seems constitutional in our Author, will scarce ever let him recognize a difference. 'Tis in the second sentence of the paragraph that he observes that 'it is *expedient* that they' (the people) 'receive directions from the state' (meaning the governing body) 'declaratory of that its will'. 'Tis in the very next sentence that we learn from him, that what it is thus '*expedient*' that the state *should* do, it

Obscured again by the next sentence—the Censor's part confounded with that of the Historian

acting, they are supreme. Because for any thing any of them do separately, or acting in bodies that are subordinate, they may any of them be punished without any disparagement to their supremacy. Not only any *may* be, but many *are*: it is what we see examples of every day.

[e] V. supra, ch. II. par. 11, ch. III. par. 7, ch. IV. par. 10.

111

does do. 'But since it is impossible in so great a multitude, to give particular injunctions to every particular man relative to each particular action, therefore,' says he 'the state establish*es*' (does *actually* establish) 'general rules' (*the* state generally, *any* state, that is to say, that one can mention, all states, in short, whatever *do* establish) 'general rules for the perpetual information and direction of *all* persons in *all* points, whether of positive or of negative duty.' Thus far our Author; so that, for ought[1] appears, whatever he could *wish* to see done in this view *is* done. Neither this state of our own, nor any other, does he wish to see do any thing more in the matter than he sees done already; nay, nor than what is sure to be done at all events: so that happily the duty he is here so forward to lay on his superiors will not sit on them very heavy. Thus far is he from having any determinate instructive meaning in that part of the paragraph in which, to appearance, and by accident, he comes nearest to it.

—Fixed and particularized— Promulgation *recommended* **11.** Not that the passage however is absolutely so remote from meaning, but that the inventive complaisance of a commentator of the admiring breed might find it pregnant with a good deal of useful matter. The design of disseminating the knowledge of the laws is glanced at by it at least, with a shew of approbation. Were our Author's writings then as sacred as they are mysterious; and were they in the number of those which stamp the seal of authority on whatever doctrines can be fastened on them; what we have read might serve as a text, from which the obligation of adopting as many measures as a man should deem subservient to that design, might, without any unexampled violence, be deduced. In this oracular passage I might find inculcated, if not *totidem syllabis*, at least *totidem literis*, as many points of legislative duty as should seem subservient to the purposes of *digestion* and *promulgation*. Thus fortified, I might press upon the legislature, and that on the score of '*duty*', to carry into execution, and that without delay, many a busy project as yet either unthought of or unheeded. I might call them with a tone of authority to their work: I [might][2] bid them go make provision forthwith for the bringing to light such scattered materials as can be found of the judicial decisions of time past,—sole and neglected materials of common law;—for the registering and publishing of all future ones as they arise;—for

---

[1] Dublin, followed by Montague and Harrison, 'aught'.
[2] This word, missing in all early editions, but evidently required by the sense, is supplied by Montague, followed by Harrison.

transforming, by a digest, the body of the common law thus com-
pleated, into statute-law;—for breaking down the whole together into
codes or parcels, as many as there are classes of persons distinguish-
ably concerned in it;—for introducing to the notice and possession of
every person his respective code:—works which public necessity cries
aloud for, at which professional interest shudders, and at which
legislative indolence[f] stands aghast.

12. All these leading points, I say, of legislative œconomy, with as
many points of detail subservient to each as a meditation not
unassiduous has suggested, I might enforce, were it necessary, by our
Author's oracular authority. For nothing less than what has been
mentioned, I trust, is necessary, in order that every man may be made
to know, in the degree in which he *might* and *ought* to be made to
know, what (in our Author's words) 'to look upon as his own, what as
another's; what absolute and what relative duties are required at his
hands; what is to be esteemed honest, dishonest, or indifferent; what
degree every man retains of his natural liberty; what he has given up as
the price of the benefits of society; and after what manner each person
is to moderate the use and exercise of those rights which the state
assigns him, in order to promote and secure the public tranquility.'[2]
In taking my leave of our Author, I finish gladly with this pleasing
peroration: a scrutinizing judgment, perhaps, would not be altogether
satisfied with it; but the ear is soothed by it, and the heart is warmed.

*The recom-
mendation
enforced by our
Author's
concluding
sentence*

13. I now put an end to the tedious and intricate war of words that
has subsisted, in a more particular manner during the course of these
two last chapters: a logomachy, wearisome enough, perhaps, and
insipid to the reader, but beyond description laborious and irksome to
the writer. What remedy? Had there been sense, I should have
attached myself to the sense: finding nothing but words; to the words I
was to attach myself, or to nothing. Had the doctrine been but *false*,
the task of exposing it would have been comparatively an easy one: but
it was what is worse, *unmeaning*; and thence it came to require all
these pains which I have been here bestowing on it: to what profit let
the reader judge.

*Necessity and use
of these verbal
criticisms*

[f] Had I seen in those days what every body has seen since, instead of *indolence* I should
have put *corruption*.—Note of the Author, 1822.[1]

---

[1] Added 1823.   [2] I Comm. 53.

'Well then',—(cries an objector)—'the task you have set yourself is at an end; and the subject of it after all, according to your own representation, teaches nothing;—according to your own shewing it is not worth attending to.—Why then bestow on it so much attention?'

In this view—To do something to instruct, but more to undeceive, the timid and admiring student:—to excite him to place more confidence in his own strength, and less in the infallibility of great names:—to help him to emancipate his judgment from the shackles of authority:—to let him see that the not understanding a discourse may as well be the writer's fault as the reader's:—to teach him to distinguish between shewy language and sound sense:—to warn him not to pay himself with words:—to shew him that what may tickle the ear, or dazzle the imagination, will not always inform the judgment:— to shew him what it is our Author can do, and has done: and what it is he has not done, and cannot do:—to dispose him rather to fast on ignorance than feed himself with error:—to let him see that with regard to an expositor of the law, our Author is not *he that should come*, but that we may be still *looking for another*.[1]—'Who then', says my objector, 'shall be that other? Yourself?—No verily.—My mission is at an end, when I have *prepared the way before him*.[2]

FINIS[3]

[1] Matthew 11:3: 'Art thou he that should come, or do we look for another?'. Cf. also Luke 7:19.

[2] Matthew 11:10 (quoting Malachi 3:1): 'Behold I send my messenger before thy face, which shall prepare thy way before thee.' Cf. also Mark 1:2 and Luke 7:27.

[3] Thus all early edns. (in 1776 and Dublin it follows the table of contents, printed at the end of the volume). Montague substitutes 'THE END'; Harrison omits both readings.

Appendix A
From the Preface to the
second edition

[This was written by Bentham in 1822, but not published.]

[two sections omitted]

III. Among the effects of the work, such as it was, was a sort of concussion, produced by it in the sort of world it belonged to: in the world of politics, but more particularly in the world of law. More particularly still, in the higher regions; the inhabitants of which, in this as in other professions, form a sort of celestial conclave, of the secrets of which, whatsoever observation is endeavoured to be made from the subjacent low grounds, is made through a medium impregnated with awe, admiration, and conjecture.

The peep here given into its mysteries will, perhaps, be found neither uninteresting nor uninstructive: it may be assistant to the grand purposes which the work itself has for its objects: objects, which may be seen containing the germ of every thing which, on the same field, has been sown by the same hand, since. A more particular object is—the throwing light into the den of the long-robed Cacus.[1] Cacus felt the light, and trembled.

The more extensive, and indeed all-comprehensive object is—the pointing attention to the imperfections which even at that time of day were seen swarming in the frame of the government, and to the ricketiness of the only foundations, in which, on the ground of argument,

[1] See 20 n. 3 above.

115

it had ever found support. No such imperfection having place but what brought profit, in some shape or other, to those among whom the power was shared,—their interest of course was, that those same imperfections should, in their whole mass, remain for ever unremoved, and therefore be, at all times, as little as possible in view.

As a basis, for all such operations as should be directed to this same object, the Fragment, at the same time, Fragment as it was, undertook to set up, and may be seen setting up accordingly, the greatest happiness of the greatest number in the character of the proper, and only proper and defensible, end of government; as the only standard, by which any apt judgment could be formed, on the propriety of any measure, or of the conduct of any person, occupied in making opposition, or giving support to it. At that time of day, so far as regards the general frame of the Government, scarcely in any one of those imperfections did the Author of the Fragment see the effect of any worse cause than inattention and prejudice: he saw not in them then, what the experience and observations of near[1] fifty years have since taught him to see in them so plainly—the elaborately organized, and anxiously cherished and guarded products of sinister interest and artifice.

Under the name of the *principle of utility*, (for that was the name adopted from David Hume),[2] the Fragment set up, as above, the *greatest happiness* principle in the character of the standard of right and wrong in the field of morality in general, and of Government in particular. In the field of Government, it found in this country the *original contract* in possession of that character.

The existence of that pretended agreement (need it now be said?) was and is a fable: authors of the fable, the whig lawyers. The invention, such as it was, had been made by them for their own purposes, and nothing could have been better contrived: for, the existence of the contract being admitted, the terms remained to be settled: and these would of course be, on each occasion, what the interest of the occasion required that they should be. It was in this offspring of falsehood and sinister interest, that the Fragment beheld the phantom, on the shoulders of which, the Revolution, that substituted Guelphs to Stuarts, and added corruption to force, had till then had its sole declared support. Against this phantom, the Fragment will be seen making declared war: the only war but one that had ever been made against it on any side, and the only war without exception that had ever been made against it, on the side and in favour of the people. Against this attack thus made, no defence has, I believe, ever

---

[1] Bowring, 'nearly'.

[2] For Hume's account of the connection between utility and morality, see his *Treatise of Human Nature*, III.iii.1 and 6, and *An Enquiry concerning the Principles of Morals*, II.ii and III.ii.

been attempted: scarcely since that time has the chimæra been seen to show itself; scarcely at any rate under its own name. Such as it was, it was the offspring of Fiction; meaning here by the word Fiction, that which is meant by it in law-language.

A fiction of law may be defined—a wilful falsehood, having for its object the stealing legislative power, by and for hands, which could not, or durst not, openly claim it,—and, but for the delusion thus produced, could not exercise it.

Thus it was that, by means of mendacity, usurpation was, on each occasion, set up, exercised, and established.

A sort of partnership was thus formed. formed, in so far as a partnership can be said to have place, between a master and his at all times removable servants: a partnership, having for its object the extracting, on joint account, and for joint benefit, out of the pockets of the people, in the largest quantity possible, the produce of the industry of the people. Monarch found force; lawyers, fraud: thus was the capital formed. Creatures of a day, and for years together, neither possessing present nor certainty of future existence, the representatives of the people, now such convenient partners, were not as yet ripe for admittance. Parties in the concern as yet but those two:—monarch and lawyers. Whatever was the fraud thus practised, partners on both sides found their account in it: interests of both provided for of course.

The monarch, not being acknowledged in the capacity of sole legislator, had every thing to gain, by suffering these his, at all times, removable creatures, thus to exercise the power belonging to that office; for, with the instrument thus constructed, and always at hand—an instrument which continually increasing experience shewed to be so fit for use—depredation and oppression might, at all times be exercised: exercised, in shapes and degrees, in which he could not have dared to exercise them by himself in a direct way, or to propose in an open way to the representatives of the people.

As little could the authors of this power-stealing system fail to find *their* account in it. For,[1] for the sake of the profit received by him as above, their master could do no otherwise than connive all along at those other lies and devices, by which depredation and oppression were acted by them for their own benefit. Here again was another source of profit to the head partner: for, in virtue and to the extent of his power of patronage,— upon each vacancy, their office, with the annexed plunderage became his; his—not to retain indeed, but at any rate *his* to give.

Mendacity is a name too soft, for falsehood thus applied; applied to such purposes, and by men so situated: for, in comparison of the suffering thus

---

[1] Bowring, '*their* account in it: since'.

117

produced, the greatest ever produced by any thing to which the word is applied in the intercourse between individual and individual, would be found inconsiderable. An operation, by which the nature and effects of it would be placed in their full and true light, is obvious and simple. Run over the field of law, as laid down in any of the books: pick out the several parts in which a fiction in any shape has been employed. The most extensively and mischievously operative will be found in Blackstone: for others, the books of judicial procedure called *books of practice*, would be to be looked at. Set down the several fictions, under the several heads they belong to; in each instance, the particular mischief to the public, together with the profit to the judge or judges of the judicatory (called the *court*, for the purpose of letting in the servants to a share of the worship paid to the master) are the articles to be looked for. If honestly looked for, in no case would there be much difficulty in finding them; in the profit made out of each fabrication, would be seen the final cause of it.

One pre-eminently serviceable and all-comprehensive effect there is, to which, if to no other, they would every one of them be found contributory. This is—the general debility thus produced in the under-standing of the deluded people:[1] for, the more prostrate that debility, the more flagrant the ulterior degree of depredation and oppression, to which they might thus be brought to submit. Of the degree of debility produced, no better measure need be given, than the fact of men's being[2] in this way made to regard falsehood, as an instrument, not only serviceable but necessary to justice.

In others this vice was not only punished all the while by these appointed guardians of virtue, but painted in its proper colours. That which is vice in all others, how could it in them be virtue? how, but that to them belonged the power of making *wrong* and *right* change natures, and determining what shall be *morality* as well as what shall be *law*; making as well the one as the other thus dependent—not on their effects on the happiness of the community at large, but on the ever-changeable good pleasure of the possessors of power, by what means soever obtained, and in what manner soever exercised. Thus, in regard to morality: and in regard to truth, the power of determining, if not what shall be truth, what, to all practical purposes, shall be taken for it. To produce ductility, produce debility. No recipe was ever more effectual: no time at which the virtue of it has been more thoroughly understood than at present. But for this, how could judges have been suffered to make law, or priests gospel, as they have been and still are?

---

[1] Bowring, 'This is general debility produced in the understanding of the deluded people'.

[2] Bowring, 'having been'.

Though in the Fragment the mask was not taken off so completely or forcibly as here, still the effects produced by any such disclosure may without much difficulty be imagined. No where, till this little work appeared, no where had there been a heart to declare—no where, perhaps, even an eye clearly to see—that, in the hands of these arbiters of every man's destiny, this pretended product of matchless wisdom—this object of veneration to the deluded multitude—had never been any thing better than a cover for rascality. By no former hand, had the gauntlet been thrown down in the face of the brotherhood: that gauntlet, which though so repeatedly offered again to learned vizards, no eye has ever yet seen the possibility of taking up.

IV. The effects produced on sinister interest—on sinister interest in these high places—by the wounds thus given to it, may, without much difficulty, be imagined. But the greatest happiness of the greatest number requires, that they should be not only imagined but proved: and this they shall now be, in so far as natural probability, aided by whatever support it may be thought to receive from the character of the narrator, can gain credence, for the indication given of a set of actings and workings, of which, for the most part, the mind, in its most secret recesses, was the theatre. These effects the reader will see in the deportments of the various personages—keepers and workers of the state engines—in relation to the present work and another by the same hand; and among them will be found the several shining lights, to which, by the conjecturists, who thereby so clearly proved themselves not to have been members of the above-mentioned conclave, the work was as above, ascribed.

He will see the great lawyers of the age—those of the one party as well as those of the other—concurring (and he will learn to judge whether it was not by concert) in a system of deportment and discourse having for its effect—(and he will judge, whether it had not also for its object)—the keeping covered up in the napkin the talents,[1] such as they were, by which the unwelcome performance had been produced. He will see the hand of a great statesman employing itself at length in the endeavour to draw them out of the napkin, and put them to use.

But for the great purposes which have been seen, never would the patience of the public have been tried by any such string of personal anecdotes, in which an insignificant individual can not but be the most prominent figure. In themselves the facts are much too trivial to afford a warrant even for the time employed in bringing them to view—a time which, considering the engagements, the performance of which has thus

---

[1] Luke 19:20, where however the parable is told with reference to 'pounds' not, as in Matthew 25:14–30 (where the napkin is not mentioned), 'talents'.

been delayed,[a] can not be thought of without remorse. One consolation, is, as already observed—(and this it is that constituted the temptation)—that, to the all-comprehensive theory of which those engagements required the establishment, these anecdotes will afford the confirmation given by particular experience.

Fundamental principles, of the Constitutional branch of the all-comprehensive Code now forming, three.

1. *End-indicating* principle, the *greatest happiness* principle.

2. *Obstacle-indicating* principle, the *universal self-preference-announcing* principle.

3. *Means-indicating* principle, the *interest-junction-prescribing* principle.[2] To him to whom the House of Commons' Votes, or even the Newspaper indications given of them, are familiar, neither a warrant nor a key will be found wanting, to[3] these denominations, laconic as they are.

Of all the great public men who will pass under review, one alone will be seen, to whom the greatest happiness principle, and the author of the Fragment, in respect of the proclamation and application made of it, was not, according to all appearance, an object of aversion. Of this aversion, the cause lay (it will be seen) in the nature of the species, of the class, and of the situation of the class on the one part, and in the nature of individuals[4] on either part. In that same situation, the conduct of any other individuals, would without material variation have been the same: the individuals in question being of both parties; men, in every sense as good as any that are ever likely to be in those same situations so long as the form of Government is what it is.

Sinister interests, two in the same breast—lawyer's interest and ruling statesman's interest: lawyer's interest, hostile to that of all suitors, and of all those who may have need to be so, that is to say—of all who are not lawyers. Ruling statesman's interest, hostile to all subjects' interest, in a form of Government, which, to the inclination common to all breasts, adds in the ruling hands adequate *power*: power, to an amount sufficient for winding up to the pitch of perfection the system of *depredation* and

---

[a] See Codification Proposal, Appendix XI. Acceptance given by the Portuguese Cortes to the offer of an all-comprehensive code.[1]

---

[1] Bowring, iv, 576, where a letter of 3 December 1821 from the Portuguese Cortes accepting Bentham's offer of a code is printed.
[2] Cf. *Constitutional Code*, in Bowring, ix, 6–7. The Ms. for this passage (U.C. xxxvi. 86–9) was written in mid-August 1822, under the heading 'Constitut[ional] Code, First Principles.' (The summer of 1822 was one of the periods when Bentham worked most actively on the early drafts of the *Constitutional Code*.)
[3] Bowring, 'for'.
[4] Bowring, 'of the individuals'.

oppression: power, by means of the *corruption* and *delusion*, which are the essence of this form of Government, in addition to that physical *force* and those means of *intimidation* and *remuneration*, which belong of necessity to *every* form of government.

Of the three confederated interests, that of the lawyer tribe is in a more particular degree mischievous: mischievous, in as much as, to their share in the common sinister interest, they add one which is peculiar to themselves, and in as much as, by the peculiar strength given to their minds by exercise, they take the lead of all the other members of the confederacy, and are the men by whose exertion whatsoever is most difficult of that which is wished to be done, is done.

And thus will be seen an exemplification of the *obstacle-indicating*—the *universal-self-preference indicating*—principle.

So long as the form of Government continues to be what it is,—not better and better, but continually worse and worse, must the condition of the people be, until the sinister sacrifice—the sacrifice of the interest of the many to the interest, joint or several, of the one or the few—shall have been consummated. In that which Austrian Italy—in that which English Ionia—in that which Ireland is—may be seen even now that which England is hastening to be.[1] Forms continuing what they are, Englishmen cannot too soon prepare themselves for being shot, sabred, hanged, or transported, at the pleasure of the placed and momentarily displaceable creatures, of a Monarch, free from *all* check, but the useless one of an Aristocracy, sharing with him in the same sinister interest. Precedents have already been established: and, by whomsoever made, whether by those who claim to make law, or by those who in the very act disclaim it, every thing for which a precedent has been made is regarded as justified. Of the several particular interests of the Aristocrat in all his shapes, including the fee-fed lawyer, and the tax-fed or rent-fed priest, all prostrate at the foot of the throne—is composed for everlastingly and unchangeably ruling interest. Opposite to the interest of the greatest number—opposite through the whole field of Government—is that same ruling interest. That which this interest requires, is—that the quantity of power, wealth, and factitious dignity, in the possession and at the disposal of the ruling few, should be at all times as great as possible. That which

---

[1] Much of northern Italy was subject to Austrian rule from the peace of Utrecht in 1713 until the unification of Italy in the mid-19th century. The Austrian regime, interrupted since Napoleon's victories in 1796–7, had been restored by the congress of Vienna in 1815. The Ionian Islands, seized by Britain from France between 1809 and 1814, were under British protection, and governed in a fairly arbitrary manner by British commissioners, from 1815 until they were transferred to Greece in 1864. Ireland, under English control since medieval times, had been brought under the direct authority of the British parliament by the 1801 Act of Union.

the interest of the subject many requires, is—that the quantity of power and wealth at the disposal of the ruling few should at all times be as small as possible: of these necessary instruments, the smallest quantity; of that worse than useless instrument—factitious dignity, not an atom: no such instrument of corruption and delusion, no such favored rival, and commodious substitute, to meritorious and really useful service: no such essentially disproportionate mode of remuneration, while, for really useful service, apt notification would afford the only remuneration, which in the shape of honour can be proportionate. Can opposition be more complete? But, to be governed by men, themselves under the dominion of an interest opposite to one's own, what is it but to be governed by one's enemies? In or out of office; possessors or expectants; Tories or Whigs; leaning most to the Monarchical side, or most to another side equally hostile to that of the people—what matter is it in which of these situations a man is, if to all the interest, he adds more than the power, of an enemy? Vain therefore—vain for ever will be all hope of relief, unless and until the form given to the Government is such, that those rulers in chief, whose particular interests are opposite to the universal interest, shall have given place to others whose particular interests have been brought into coincidence with that same universal interest; in a word, till the *interest-junction-prescribing* principle, as above, shall have been carried into effect. In the Anglo-American United States, this problem—has it not been solved?

———————

[remaining sections omitted]

———————

Appendix B
From a draft Preface

[This is a draft preface written at about the time Bentham wrote the
Fragment but left in manuscript.]

To purge the science of the poison introduced into it by him[1] and those
who write as he does, I know but of one remedy; and that is by *Definition*,
perpetual and regular definition, the grand prescription of those great
physicians of the mind, Helvetius and before him Locke. Useful and
legitimate definition which (not like his)[a] explains terms less familiar by
terms more familiar, terms more abstract by terms less abstract, terms
with a larger assemblage of simple ideas belonging to them, by terms with
an assemblage less extensive.

The reader is not to expect to see these Definitions[2] supported by
authorities. The writers we have seen hitherto, Coke, Hale, Hawkins,
Wood,[3] the list ending with our Author, very good Lawyers as Lawyers

---

[a] *His definitions* strings of identical propositions or explaining *ignotum per ignotius*.

---

[1] Blackstone.

[2] Ms. orig. 'principles'. This paragraph has the marginal heading 'Definitions here
given' – i.e. Bentham's own definitions.

[3] The *Reports* of Sir Edward Coke (1552–1634), Chief Justice of the Common
Pleas and later of the King's Bench, were first published in French 1600–15 and
in English 1656–9. Sir Matthew Hale (1609–76) became Lord Chief Justice of
the King's Bench in 1671. William Hawkins (1673–1746) published *A Treatise of
the Pleas of the Crown* in 1716. Thomas Wood (1661–1722) was the author of *An
Institute of the Laws of England, or The Laws of England in their Natural Order
according to Common Use.* First published in 1720, this had gone into a tenth
edition by 1772. It remained the leading comprehensive survey of English law
until superseded by Blackstone's *Commentaries.*

went, have been very poor philosophers. Locke (the Father of intellectual science) had not yet spoken[1] to them, or had spoken to them in vain. It is not much wonder if he should have spoken to them in vain. Few works show greater marks of the want of these precautions than his own on Government.[2] They were content as most men are content to ring the changes upon the words they have been used to, without knowing what they meant by them. Nothing has been, nothing will be, nothing ever can be done on the subject of Law that deserves the name of Science, till that universal precept of Locke, enforced, exemplified and particularly applied to the moral branch of science by Helvetius, be steadily pursued, 'Define your words'. It is true, it is not for every man in matters of moral science to define his words. It is what a little understanding can not: a timid heart dare not do it. Men who, fettered by engagements, have abjured the right of thinking and find it their interest to persist in their abjuration, start from a task like this with loathing and with terror. They dare not venture into the recesses of the science for fear of spying out deformities which to correct would be mortal to their hopes: helpless victims of a blind and antiquated policy, they dare not look their own notions in the face: they dare not strike out those hidden | |[3] where[4] they would elicit[5] hidden lights that would appall them with the prospect of the absurdities they have swallowed and which they must continue to swallow, unless they would forfeit all hopes of pleasing those whom the petty interest of their fortunes necessitates them to please. We are thus far advanced in this country towards the development of moral truths (those moral and political truths which the principle of utility incloses in its bosom): the spirit of the people offers them immunity, but it is problematical at least whether the promises[?] of the rulers offer them reward.

I don't know how it may prove with the reader: but I can promise him, that the writer has again and again been most heartily sick of the Logical and Metaphysical researches into which he has been led in quest [of] lights to dissipate if possible the confusion in which our Author has involved the subject, and for materials to pave the way to a somewhat less inaccurate conception of it than he has given us.

I speak with respect to the judgment that is passed (when any is passed) on a subject, or the particular light in which it is holden up, where no formal judgment is pronounced: for as to saying that there is such a

---

[1] Ms. 'Spoke'.
[2] John Locke, *Two Treatises of Government* (1690).
[3] Though no gap in fact appears at this point in the Ms., it seems clear that a word is missing.
[4] Ms. 'were'.
[5] Ms. orig. 'encounter'.

Statute where there is one, or that such a point of Common law is established, when all the world is agreed about it, this sort of discourse, of which the greatest part of the book is necessarily composed, will stand wherever it is placed.[1] That we can get a notion from him how things are (which is not always) it[?] is well: but that his judgment is no safe standard for us of what they ought to be.

Had he confined himself to the giving his notion of things as they are, or to giving his notion of what they ought to be without shutting the door against enquiry[?],[2] he would never have heard from me in this manner. We would have joined hands and jogged on together in our enquiries in peace and good fellowship, if he had been a man a plain but free enquirer after truth could have joined hands with. 'Tis not for being in the wrong himself, but for the little anxiety he has shewn that others should be, or rather I might say the great anxiety he has shewn to prevent them from being in the right.

If something in point of sense were said, were that something false, one might sit down seriously and quietly to examine: but the great vexation is to find nothing said in so many words and to find that vexation occurring at every step: so that the greatest part of what is said is just so much worse than nothing.[3] It is curious that a writer who is so eager to have men punished for being at variance with him in their discourses, can scarce ever keep clear from being at variance with himself for two pages together: instance Sanction in p. 54 attributed and denied to human Laws.[4] His nomenclature [is] like a weathercock: you never meet with the same term twice together in the same place. In the midst of all this darkness, here and there a position makes it appearance that is intelligible: and as sure almost as it is intelligible it will be found false.

The public may perhaps one day see an attempt to build up something in its room. But at any rate it will be of service to have demolished error, though the ground should remain sometime vacant. Upon ground that is already covered, and that groans beneath the load that's laid on it, clearing away the rubbish is a necessary step preparatory to building. Simple ignorance is a greater friend than every one is aware to knowledge. It gives the reins to inquiry when curiosity gives the spur: nor fails curiosity to give it when interest gives the nod: a pressing and recognized public interest which includes all private interests. Error overturns the

---

[1] At this point in the Ms., the following incomplete sentence occurs: 'To set a mark of censure or approbation | |'.

[2] Ms. 'enquired[?]'.

[3] This sentence is immediately preceded by the following incomplete sentence, which has the marginal heading 'Word-catching': 'word-catching – a business equally futile and obnoxious – but having taken much pains to find a sense in it and finding none a man must catch at words or catch at nothing.'

[4] I Comm. 54.

mind motionless in quagmires; or hurries[?] it out of the road over Rocks and Precipices.

Nor does the filling up of a vacancy thus made in the territories of knowledge rest exclusively on him who made it. In this great common a void space by whomsoever made or left, invites the first adventurer to come in and build.

With respect to my own labour, whatever else is wanting, two things I can affirm have not been wanting, *solicitude*[1] and *plain-dealing*.[2] Solicitude to discover what it might be of use to know, plain-dealing to declare it. 'Tis not this or that class of men, much less this or that individual, I have studied to please, but the great body of the public: and so to please as may be done by the application not of flattery to their affections, but of instruction so far as my diligence can do it to their understanding. My primary aim is the emancipating their judicial faculties from those shackles in which it is the tendency of our Author's instruction to hold[?] them bound[?].[3] They will then be free to take their own course with us ... with the grand principle of utility for their guide. The honour of assisting them in their progress is, for the present at least but a secondary hope. If in judging between both[4] they learnt but to speculate for themselves, I care not with what rigour they judge me. If any thing here said can serve to coax them from that sheep-like habit, in no class of men so inveterate as in Lawyers, of blindly treading in the footsteps of a leader, I shall think it my gain, as does the experienced master, when by laying himself open now and then to the pushes of his Pupil, he teaches him to discover the secret of his strength.

[1] Ms. orig. preferred to alt. *'industry'*, which Bentham does not adopt below.

[2] Ms. orig. *'unreserve'*.

[3] The following phrases, which have the marginal heading 'Demerits—summing up', but for which no close context has been found elsewhere, may not be inapposite here:

> That when we ask of him a fish, he should cheat us with a serpent. That he should so often be the divine when he should be the politician, the Orator when he should be the Preceptor, the Copyist when he should be the Author, the Panegyrist when he should be the Censor, the subject, not to say the slave, when he should be the citizen.

The opening phrase refers to Matthew 7:10: 'Or if he ask a fish, will he give him a serpent?' (also Luke 11:11).

[4] I.e. between Blackstone and Bentham.

Index

Only the Introduction to the book and Bentham's own text and footnotes are indexed.